BLACK expressions

2005 Calendar

CELEBRATING
A HALF CENTURY OF
CIVIL RIGHTS MILESTONES

Name

Address

City   State   Zip

Telephone

E-Mail

From the desk of Carol M. Mackey

Dear Member,

On behalf of Black Expressions Book Club, I'd like to personally thank you for your continued support. Your membership and support of African American books is greatly appreciated. That's why it gives me great pleasure to present this members-only exclusive 2005 desk calendar!

The Black Expressions 2005 desk calendar is one of our most popular items—members love it and it makes a great gift. This year, we celebrate and pay homage to the Civil Rights Movement and its contributors. It was one of the most tumultuous eras in our history, but necessary to our progress and growth as a people. This desk calendar is a testament to the contributions of the "bold soldiers" who stood on the front lines and battled for our freedom and equality. And, it's a great place to keep all your important dates, appointments, names, and numbers, so enjoy it all year long.

Moving onward and upward in 2005,

Carol

Carol M. Mackey
Senior Editor

2005 Planner

JANUARY

S	M	T	W	T	F	S
						1
2	3	4	5	6	7	8
9	10	11	12	13	14	15
16	17	18	19	20	21	22
23/30	24/31	25	26	27	28	29

FEBRUARY

S	M	T	W	T	F	S
		1	2	3	4	5
6	7	8	9	10	11	12
13	14	15	16	17	18	19
20	21	22	23	24	25	26
27	28					

MARCH

S	M	T	W	T	F	S
		1	2	3	4	5
6	7	8	9	10	11	12
13	14	15	16	17	18	19
20	21	22	23	24	25	26
27	28	29	30	31		

2005 Planner

APRIL

S	M	T	W	T	F	S
					1	2
3	4	5	6	7	8	9
10	11	12	13	14	15	16
17	18	19	20	21	22	23
24	25	26	27	28	29	30

MAY

S	M	T	W	T	F	S
1	2	3	4	5	6	7
8	9	10	11	12	13	14
15	16	17	18	19	20	21
22	23	24	25	26	27	28
29	30	31				

JUNE

S	M	T	W	T	F	S
			1	2	3	4
5	6	7	8	9	10	11
12	13	14	15	16	17	18
19	20	21	22	23	24	25
26	27	28	29	30		

2005 Planner

JULY

S	M	T	W	T	F	S
					1	2
3	4	5	6	7	8	9
10	11	12	13	14	15	16
17	18	19	20	21	22	23
24/31	25	26	27	28	29	30

AUGUST

S	M	T	W	T	F	S
	1	2	3	4	5	6
7	8	9	10	11	12	13
14	15	16	17	18	19	20
21	22	23	24	25	26	27
28	29	30	31			

SEPTEMBER

S	M	T	W	T	F	S
				1	2	3
4	5	6	7	8	9	10
11	12	13	14	15	16	17
18	19	20	21	22	23	24
25	26	27	28	29	30	

2005 Planner

OCTOBER

S	M	T	W	T	F	S
						1
2	3	4	5	6	7	8
9	10	11	12	13	14	15
16	17	18	19	20	21	22
23/30	24/31	25	26	27	28	29

NOVEMBER

S	M	T	W	T	F	S
		1	2	3	4	5
6	7	8	9	10	11	12
13	14	15	16	17	18	19
20	21	22	23	24	25	26
27	28	29	30			

DECEMBER

S	M	T	W	T	F	S
				1	2	3
4	5	6	7	8	9	10
11	12	13	14	15	16	17
18	19	20	21	22	23	24
25	26	27	28	29	30	31

BIRTHDAYS & ANNIVERSARIES

JANUARY

FEBRUARY

MARCH

JULY

AUGUST

SEPTEMBER

BIRTHDAYS & ANNIVERSARIES

APRIL

MAY

JUNE

OCTOBER

NOVEMBER

DECEMBER

27 Monday
2ND DAY OF KWANZAA

8AM

9

10

11

12

1PM

2

3

4

5

6

28 Tuesday
3RD DAY OF KWANZAA

8AM

9

10

11

12

1PM

2

3

4

5

6

29 Wednesday
4TH DAY OF KWANZAA

8AM

9

10

11

12

1PM

2

3

4

5

6

"NO TIE BINDS MEN CLOSER"

EVEN ITS CHILDREN KNOW THAT THE SOUTH IS IN TROUBLE. No one has to tell them; no words said aloud. To them, it is a vague thing weaving in and out of their play, like a ghost haunting an old graveyard or whispers after the household sleeps—fleeting mystery, vague menace, to which each responds in his own way. Some learn to screen out all except the soft and the soothing; others deny even as they see plainly, and hear. But all know that under quiet words and warmth and laughter, under the slow ease and tender concern about small matters, there is a heavy burden on all of us and as heavy a refusal to confess it. The children know

this "trouble" is bigger than they, bigger than their family, bigger than their church, so big that people turn away from its size. They have seen it flash out like lightning and shatter a town's peace, have felt it tear up all they believe in. They have measured its giant strength and they feel weak when they remember.

This haunted childhood belongs to every southerner. Many of us run away from it but we come back like a hurt animal to its wound, or a murderer to the scene of his sin. The human heart dares not stay away too long from that which hurt it most. There is a return journey to anguish that

30 Thursday
5TH DAY OF KWANZAA

8AM

9

10

11

12

1PM

2

3

4

5

6

31 Friday
NEW YEAR'S EVE
6TH DAY OF KWANZAA

8AM

9

10

11

12

1PM

2

3

4

5

6

1 Saturday
NEW YEAR'S DAY
7TH DAY OF KWANZAA
ABRAHAM LINCOLN ISSUES THE
EMANCIPATION PROCLAMATION, 1863

2 Sunday
John Hope Franklin born 1915

few of us are released from making.

We who were born in the South call this mesh of feeling and memory "loyalty." We think of it sometimes as "love." We identify with the South's trouble as if we, individually, were responsible for all of it. We defend the sins and sorrows of three hundred years as if each sin had been committed by us alone and each sorrow had cut across our heart. We are as hurt at criticism of our region as if our own name were called aloud by the critic. We have known guilt without understanding it, and there is no tie that binds men closer to the past and each other than that.

—Lillian Smith

Lillian Smith, *Killers of the Dream* (New York: W.W. Norton, 1949).

DECEMBER

S	M	T	W	T	F	S
			1	2	3	4
5	6	7	8	9	10	11
12	13	14	15	16	17	18
19	20	21	22	23	24	25
26	27	28	29	30	31	

JANUARY

S	M	T	W	T	F	S
						1
2	3	4	5	6	7	8
9	10	11	12	13	14	15
16	17	18	19	20	21	22
23/30	24/31	25	26	27	28	29

3 Monday
Alonzo J. Ransier born 1834

8AM

9

10

11

12

1PM

2

3

4

5

6

4 Tuesday
Selena S. Butler born 1872

8AM

9

10

11

12

1PM

2

3

4

5

6

5 Wednesday

8AM

9

10

11

12

1PM

2

3

4

5

6

"THIS IS GOD'S MOVEMENT"

(SOUTHERN CHRISTIAN LEADERSHIP CONFERENCE FORMED JANUARY 1957)

Its clerical leadership made SCLC uniquely equipped to communicate with ordinary blacks. For the most part excluded from politics, blacks had long used religion to sublimate or disguise their political aspirations. SCLC's leaders clothed political ideas in a religious phraseology that blacks readily understood and used Christian tenets to give the civil rights movement a divine sanction. As Ralph Abernathy, SCLC's vice-president, put it, "This is God's movement. There can be *no* injunction against God." Being preachers, they were adept at combining exhortation with entertainment, and provided what Bayard Rustin called "an emotional dimension to whip up the enthusiasm of the people." SCLC's identification with the church was invaluable when it came to organizing local protests, for churchgoers attended its mass meetings as they would Sunday services.

6 Thursday

8AM

9

10

11

12

1PM

2

3

4

5

6

7 Friday

8AM

9

10

11

12

1PM

2

3

4

5

6

8 Saturday

9 Sunday

JANUARY

S	M	T	W	T	F	S
						1
2	3	4	5	6	7	8
9	10	11	12	13	14	15
16	17	18	19	20	21	22
23/30	24/31	25	26	27	28	29

FEBRUARY

S	M	T	W	T	F	S
		1	2	3	4	5
6	7	8	9	10	11	12
13	14	15	16	17	18	19
20	21	22	23	24	25	26
27	28					

10 Monday

8AM

9

10

11

12

1PM

2

3

4

5

6

11 Tuesday

8AM

9

10

11

12

1PM

2

3

4

5

6

12 Wednesday

8AM

9

10

11

12

1PM

2

3

4

5

6

"AN ORGANIC INTELLECTUAL OF THE FIRST ORDER"

King is the exemplary figure of the first stage of the black freedom movement in the sixties not only because he was its gifted and courageous leader or simply because of his organizational achievements, but, more important, because he consolidated the most progressive potential available in the black Southern community at that time: the cultural potency of prophetic black churches, the skills of engaged black preachers, trade-unionists and professionals, and the spirit of rebellion and resistance of the black working poor and underclass. In this sense, King was an organic intellectual of the first order—a highly educated and informed thinker with organic links to ordinary folk. Despite his petit bourgeois origins, his deep roots in the black church gave him direct access to the life-worlds of the majority of black Southerners. In addition, his education at Morehouse College, Crozier Theological Seminary and Boston University provided him with opportunities to reflect upon various anticolonial struggles around the world, especially those in India and Ghana, and also entitled him to respect and admiration in the eyes of black people, including the "old," black, middle class (composed primarily of teachers and preachers). Last, his Christian outlook and personal temperament facilitated relations with progressive nonblack people, thereby insuring openness to potential allies.

—Cornel West

13 Thursday
Charlotte E. Ray born 1850

14 Friday
Julian Bond born 1940

15 Saturday
Martin Luther King Jr. born 1929

13 Thursday	14 Friday
8AM	8AM
9	9
10	10
11	11
12	12
1PM	1PM
2	2
3	3
4	4
5	5
6	6

16 Sunday

JANUARY

S	M	T	W	T	F	S
						1
2	3	4	5	6	7	8
9	10	11	12	13	14	15
16	17	18	19	20	21	22
23/30	24/31	25	26	27	28	29

FEBRUARY

S	M	T	W	T	F	S
		1	2	3	4	5
6	7	8	9	10	11	12
13	14	15	16	17	18	19
20	21	22	23	24	25	26
27	28					

Cornel West, *Keeping the Faith: Philosophy and Race in America* (New York: Routledge, 1993), 273.

17 Monday
MARTIN LUTHER KING JR. DAY
Muhammad Ali born 1942

8AM

9

10

11

12

1PM

2

3

4

5

6

18 Tuesday

8AM

9

10

11

12

1PM

2

3

4

5

6

19 Wednesday

8AM

9

10

11

12

1PM

2

3

4

5

6

"WE CAN NEVER BE SATISFIED"

The whirlwinds of revolt will continue to shake the foundations of our nation until the bright day of justice emerges. But there is something that I must say to my people who stand on the warm threshold which leads into the palace of justice. In the process of gaining our rightful place we must not be guilty of wrongful deeds. Let us not seek to satisfy our thirst for freedom by drinking from the cup of bitterness and hatred.

We must forever conduct our struggle on the high plane of dignity and discipline. We must not allow our creative protest to degenerate into physical violence. Again and again we must rise to the majestic heights of meeting physical force with soul force.

The marvelous new militancy which has engulfed the Negro community must not lead us to distrust of all white people, for many of our white brothers, as evidenced by their presence here today, have come to realize that their destiny is tied up with our destiny and their freedom is inextricably bound to our freedom. We cannot walk alone. And as we walk, we must make the pledge that we shall

20 Thursday

8AM
_____
_____
9
_____
_____
10
_____
_____
11
_____
_____
12
_____
_____
1PM
_____
_____
2
_____
_____
3
_____
_____
4
_____
_____
5
_____
_____
6
_____
_____

21 Friday

8AM
_____
_____
9
_____
_____
10
_____
_____
11
_____
_____
12
_____
_____
1PM
_____
_____
2
_____
_____
3
_____
_____
4
_____
_____
5
_____
_____
6
_____
_____

22 Saturday

_____
_____
_____
_____
_____
_____
_____
_____

23 Sunday

24TH AMENDMENT ELIMINATES POLL TAX
ON FEDERAL ELECTIONS, 1964
Amanda Smith born 1837
Paul Robeson dies 1976

_____
_____
_____
_____
_____

always march ahead. We cannot turn back. There are those who are asking the devotees of civil rights, "When will you be satisfied?" We can never be satisfied as long as a Negro is the victim of all the unspeakable horrors of police brutality. We can never be satisfied as long as our bodies, heavy with the fatigue of travel, cannot gain lodging in the motels of the highways and the hotels of the cities. We can never be satisfied as long as a Negro in Mississippi cannot vote and a Negro in New York believes he has nothing for which to vote. No, no, we are not satisfied, and we will not be satisfied until justice rolls down like waters and righteousness like a mighty stream.

—Martin Luther King Jr.'s Most Famous Speech,
"I Have A Dream," Delivered on the Steps of the
Lincoln Memorial in Washington, D.C., August 28, 1963

JANUARY

S	M	T	W	T	F	S
						1
2	3	4	5	6	7	8
9	10	11	12	13	14	15
16	17	18	19	20	21	22
23/30	24/31	25	26	27	28	29

FEBRUARY

S	M	T	W	T	F	S
		1	2	3	4	5
6	7	8	9	10	11	12
13	14	15	16	17	18	19
20	21	22	23	24	25	26
27	28					

24 Monday
Arthur Schomburg born 1874
Thurgood Marshall dies 1993

8AM

9

10

11

12

1PM

2

3

4

5

6

25 Tuesday

8AM

9

10

11

12

1PM

2

3

4

5

6

26 Wednesday
May Miller born 1899
Angela Y. Davis born 1944

8AM

9

10

11

12

1PM

2

3

4

5

6

"PRIVILEGES AND PRIORITIES ... SIMPLY BECAUSE THEY WERE WHITE"

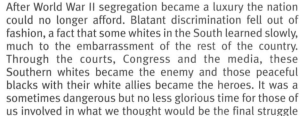

After World War II segregation became a luxury the nation could no longer afford. Blatant discrimination fell out of fashion, a fact that some whites in the South learned slowly, much to the embarrassment of the rest of the country. Through the courts, Congress and the media, these Southern whites became the enemy and those peaceful blacks with their white allies became the heroes. It was a sometimes dangerous but no less glorious time for those of us involved in what we thought would be the final struggle for civil rights.

But while the Jim Crow signs came down after prolonged battles in the courts and on the streets, society quickly devised means to limit the substantive value of the pro-civil rights decisions and the new civil rights laws enacted during the 1960s. The frustrations engendered by these barriers led to the Black Power movement in the middle and late 1960s, a phenomenon that alienated some whites, and the riots in Watts and other places that turned off still more. The real disenchantment came when whites began to recognize that civil rights for blacks meant more than condemning the use of fire hoses and police dogs on peacefully protesting children in a Deep South town. It meant, as well, giving up privileges and priorities long available to whites simply because they were white.

—Derrick Bell

27 Thursday

8AM

9

10

11

12

1PM

2

3

4

5

6

28 Friday

8AM

9

10

11

12

1PM

2

3

4

5

6

29 Saturday

30 Sunday

JANUARY						
S	M	T	W	T	F	S
						1
2	3	4	5	6	7	8
9	10	11	12	13	14	15
16	17	18	19	20	21	22
23/30	24/31	25	26	27	28	29

FEBRUARY						
S	M	T	W	T	F	S
		1	2	3	4	5
6	7	8	9	10	11	12
13	14	15	16	17	18	19
20	21	22	23	24	25	26
27	28					

Derrick Bell, "The Freedom of Employment Act," *Nation* 238, no. 20 (1994), 713.

31 Monday
Jackie Robinson born 1919
Benjamin L. Hooks born 1925

1 Tuesday
SIT-IN BEGINS AT WOOLWORTH'S IN
GREENSBORO, NORTH CAROLINA, 1960

2 Wednesday

31 Monday	1 Tuesday	2 Wednesday
8AM	8AM	8AM
9	9	9
10	10	10
11	11	11
12	12	12
1PM	1PM	1PM
2	2	2
3	3	3
4	4	4
5	5	5
6	6	6

NOT JUST ANOTHER DAY AT THE LOCAL WOOLWORTH'S

Inspired by the praxis of King, MIA [Montgomery Improvement Association], and SCLC [Southern Christian Leadership Conference]—as well as the sit-in techniques employed by the Congress of Racial Equality—four black freshmen students at North Carolina Agricultural and Technical College in Greensboro staged a sit-in at the local Woolworth's on February 1, 1960. Within a week, their day-to-day sit-in had been joined by black and white students from the Women's College of the University of North Carolina, North Carolina College and Duke University.

Within two weeks, the sit-in movement had spread to fifteen other cities in Virginia, Tennessee and South Carolina. Within two months, there were sit-ins in seventy-eight cities. By the end of 1960 over fifty thousand people throughout the South had participated in sit-in demonstrations, with over twenty-five percent of the black students in predominantly black colleges participating. In short, young black people (and some progressive white people) had taken seriously King's techniques of nonviolence and the spirit of resistance.

3 Thursday
15TH AMENDMENT RATIFIED, 1830

8AM

9

10

11

12

1PM

2

3

4

5

6

4 Friday
Rosa Parks born 1913

8AM

9

10

11

12

1PM

2

3

4

5

6

5 Saturday

6 Sunday
Anne Spencer born 1882

This spontaneous rebellion of young black people against the southern taboo of black and white people eating together in public places exemplified a major component in the first stage of the black freedom movement: the emergence of politicized, black parvenu, petit-bourgeois students. The students, especially young preachers and Christian activists, prefigured the disposition and orientation of the vastly increasing number of black college students in the sixties; they would give first priority to social activism and justify their newly acquired privileges by personal risk and sacrifice.

—Cornel West

Cornel West, *Keeping the Faith: Philosophy and Race in America* (New York: Routledge, 1993), 274-275.

FEBRUARY

S	M	T	W	T	F	S
		1	2	3	4	5
6	7	8	9	10	11	12
13	14	15	16	17	18	19
20	21	22	23	24	25	26
27	28					

MARCH

S	M	T	W	T	F	S
		1	2	3	4	5
6	7	8	9	10	11	12
13	14	15	16	17	18	19
20	21	22	23	24	25	26
27	28	29	30	31		

7 Monday
Frederick Douglass born 1817?

8AM

9

10

11

12

1PM

2

3

4

5

6

8 Tuesday

8AM

9

10

11

12

1PM

2

3

4

5

6

9 Wednesday
ASH WEDNESDAY

8AM

9

10

11

12

1PM

2

3

4

5

6

LOOK WHAT GREW OUT OF OUR
✳✳✳✳✳✳✳ IMPATIENCE ✳✳✳✳✳✳✳

From the 1930s to 1950s, [Charles Hamilton] Houston, [Thurgood] Marshall, and an increasing number of black and white lawyers cooperating with the NAACP/LDF [National Association for the Advancement of Colored People Legal Defense Fund] in a wide variety of locales plotted a careful strategy to defeat legal segregation. In general, the LDF focused on destroying the legal basis for the "separate but equal" doctrine put forward in the U.S. Supreme Court's *Plessy vs. Ferguson* decision (1896). These LDF lawyers challenged salary discrepancies between black and white public school teachers, racial discrimination in higher education, the exclusion of African Americans from jury duty, and black disenfranchisement in the southern states. The LDF achieved a victorious climax in 1954 with the U.S. Supreme Court's *Brown vs. Board of Education* decision, declaring legal segregation in public education unconstitutional. Unfortunately, the Supreme Court did not order the immediate desegregation of public schools in *Brown II* (1955), and this allowed obstructionist local school boards and cooperating circuit courts to delay integration seemingly (to many at the time) indefinitely. Out of this impatience grew other approaches to pursue equal rights; and these tactics, campaigns and activities became the Civil Rights Movement.

—Will Sarvis

10 Thursday

8AM

9

10

11

12

1PM

2

3

4

5

6

11 Friday

8AM

9

10

11

12

1PM

2

3

4

5

6

12 Saturday

NAACP FOUNDED, 1909
Fannie Barrier Williams born 1855

13 Sunday

Emmett J. Scott born 1873

FEBRUARY

S	M	T	W	T	F	S
		1	2	3	4	5
6	7	8	9	10	11	12
13	14	15	16	17	18	19
20	21	22	23	24	25	26
27	28					

MARCH

S	M	T	W	T	F	S
		1	2	3	4	5
6	7	8	9	10	11	12
13	14	15	16	17	18	19
20	21	22	23	24	25	26
27	28	29	30	31		

Will S... Leaders in the Court and Community: Z. Alexander Looby, Avon N. Williams, Jr., and the Legal Fight for Civ... ts in Tennessee, 1940-1970," *Journal of African American History* 88, no. 1 (2003), 45-46.

14 Monday
VALENTINE'S DAY
Richard Allen born 1760

8AM

9

10

11

12

1PM

2

3

4

5

6

15 Tuesday

8AM

9

10

11

12

1PM

2

3

4

5

6

16 Wednesday

8AM

9

10

11

12

1PM

2

3

4

5

6

"MANY OF THE FBI'S TACTICS WERE CLEARLY INTENDED TO FOSTER VIOLENCE"

One word that comes up again and again in the FBI documents is "neutralization." That is a military term, a war term. They were talking about war against people who were simply trying to exercise rights and stand up for justice. The targets included such groups as the Southern Christian Leadership Council, the Revolutionary Action Movement, the Deacons for Defense, the Black Panther Party, Students for a Democratic Society, Nation of Islam, Republic of New Africa, and the National Lawyers Guild. The FBI organized a vast network of political spies who infiltrated thousands of organizations, and trained and coordinated similar operations by other law enforcement agencies at every level of government. The information gathered by informants was augmented by illegal wiretaps, letter openings, burglaries of homes and offices, secret examination of bank records, physical surveillance, and arranged murders.

By 1969 the Black Panther Party had become a primary focus of the program, and was ultimately the target of 233 of the total 295 authorized black nationalist COINTELPRO [counterintelligence program] operations. Although the claimed purpose of the Bureau's COINTELPRO action was to "prevent violence," many of the FBI's tactics were clearly

1[ ] Thursday
M[ ] Frances Berry born 1938
[ ]y P. Newton born 1942

8AM

9

10

11

12

1PM

2

3

4

5

6

18 Friday
8AM

9

10

11

12

1PM

2

3

4

5

6

19 Saturday
Lugenia Burns Hope born 1871

20 Sunday

inten[ ] to foster violence. Some of these were assassinations, false impris[ ]ment, and provocateur activities. Such actions demonstrate that the chief [ ]estigative branch of the federal government, which was charged by law w[ ] investigating crimes and criminal conduct, itself engaged in lawless tactic[ ]nd responded to deep-seated social problems by fomenting violence and u[ ]est. Many organizations and individuals did not survive the FBI neutr[ ]ation program. Some were outright destroyed, some seriously weak[ ]d and destabilized. Many were unjustly imprisoned; others were driven [ ]derground. Some were outright murdered.

—Susie Day and Laura Whitehorn

Susie D[ ] and Laura Whitehorn, "Human Rights in the United States: The Unfinished Story of Political Prisone[ ] nd COINTELPRO," *New Political Science* 23, *no. 2* (2001), 287.

FEBRUARY

S	M	T	W	T	F	S
		1	2	3	4	5
6	7	8	9	10	11	12
13	14	15	16	17	18	19
20	21	22	23	24	25	26
27	28					

MARCH

S	M	T	W	T	F	S
		1	2	3	4	5
6	7	8	9	10	11	12
13	14	15	16	17	18	19
20	21	22	23	24	25	26
27	28	29	30	31		

21 Monday
PRESIDENTS' DAY
Barbara Jordan born 1936
Malcolm X dies 1965

8AM

9

10

11

12

1PM

2

3

4

5

6

22 Tuesday

8AM

9

10

11

12

1PM

2

3

4

5

6

23 Wednesday
W.E.B. Du Bois born 1868

8AM

9

10

11

12

1PM

2

3

4

5

6

"AN UNMISTAKABLE COMMON DENOMINATOR"

BY THE SECOND DECADE OF THE TWENTIETH CENTURY, the mass movement, headed by Marcus Garvey, proclaimed in its Declaration of Rights that Black people should not hesitate to disobey discriminatory laws. Moreover, the Declaration announced, they should utilize all means available to them, legal or illegal, to defend themselves from legalized terror as well as Ku Klux Klan violence. During the era of intense activity around civil rights issues, systematic disobedience of oppressive laws was a primary tactic. The sit-ins were organized transgressions of racist legislation.

All of these historical instances involving the overt violations of the laws of the land converge around an unmistakable common denominator. At stake there has been the collective welfare and survival of a people. There is a distinct and qualitative difference between one breaking a law for one's own individual self-interest and violating it in the interests of a class or a people whose oppression is expressed either directly or indirectly through that particular law. The former might be called a criminal (though in many instances he is a victim), but the latter, as a reformist or revolutionary, is interested in social change. Captured, he or she is a political prisoner.

—Angela Y. Davis

24 Thursday

ANGELA Y. DAVIS RELEASED AFTER SERVING
16 MONTHS IN PRISON, 1972

8AM

9

10

11

12

1PM

2

3

4

5

6

25 Friday

8AM

9

10

11

12

1PM

2

3

4

5

6

26 Saturday

27 Sunday

Angelina Weld Grimké born 1880
Mabel Keaton Staupers born 1890

FEBRUARY

S	M	T	W	T	F	S
		1	2	3	4	5
6	7	8	9	10	11	12
13	14	15	16	17	18	19
20	21	22	23	24	25	26
27	28					

MARCH

S	M	T	W	T	F	S
		1	2	3	4	5
6	7	8	9	10	11	12
13	14	15	16	17	18	19
20	21	22	23	24	25	26
27	28	29	30	31		

Angela Y. Davis, "Political Prisoners, Prison and Black Liberation," in Angela Y. Davis, *If They Come in the Morning: Voices of Resistance* (New York: Signet Classics, 1971), 29-30.

28 Monday

1 Tuesday

Blanche K. Bruce born 1841

2 Wednesday

28 Monday	1 Tuesday	2 Wednesday
8AM	8AM	8AM
9	9	9
10	10	10
11	11	11
12	12	12
1PM	1PM	1PM
2	2	2
3	3	3
4	4	4
5	5	5
6	6	6

✳ THE NEW CHAMPION ✳ WHO SPOKE UP FOR US

THE NEW CHAMPION SHOOK UP THE WORLD, by proclaiming his adherence to the Nation of Islam/Black Muslims, and that henceforth he would be known as Muhammad Ali. By renouncing his "slave name," he had renounced the perceived limitations of his social and professional status and aspirations. Before him boxers did not concern themselves with politics, religion and social justice—they were deemed to be "all brawn and no brains" who were too dim to grasp the meaning of such concepts. This titleholder, though, was witty, intelligent and committed: his mind and mouth expressed themselves as clearly as his fists. In him the Africans of the Diaspora gained a representative who spoke up for them—and he was popular and respected beyond the fistic fraternity.

—Clayton Goodwin

FEBRUARY-MARCH 2005

3 Thursday

8AM

9

10

11

12

1PM

2

3

4

5

6

4 Friday

8AM

9

10

11

12

1PM

2

3

4

5

6

5 Saturday

NATION OF ISLAM LEADER
ELIJAH MUHAMMAD ANNOUNCES CASSIUS
CLAY'S NEW NAME, "MUHAMMAD ALI," 1964

6 Sunday

Clayton Goodwin, "No Vietnamese Ever Called Me a Nigger," *New African*, no. 428 (2004), 64-67.

7 Monday
BLOODY SUNDAY, 1965

8AM

9

10

11

12

1PM

2

3

4

5

6

8 Tuesday

8AM

9

10

11

12

1PM

2

3

4

5

6

9 Wednesday

8AM

9

10

11

12

1PM

2

3

4

5

6

"THOSE WHO WALKED BY FAITH . . . LED US ALL TO A BETTER TOMORROW"

Selma became a seminal moment in the history of our country. On this bridge, America's long march to freedom met a roadblock of violent resistance. But the marchers, thank God, would not take a detour on the road to freedom.

By 1965, their will had already been steeled by triumph and tragedy, by the breaking of the color line at Ole Miss, the historic March on Washington, the assassinations of Medgar Evers, Malcolm X, and President Kennedy, the bombing deaths of four little black girls at the 16th Street Baptist Church in Birmingham, the Mississippi Freedom Summer, the passage of the Civil Rights Act of 1964.

On this Bloody Sunday, about 600 foot soldiers, some of whom, thankfully, remain with us today, absorbed with uncommon dignity the unbridled force of racism, putting their lives on the line for that most basic American right: the simple right to vote, a right which already had been long guaranteed and long denied.

Here in Dallas County, there were no black elected officials because only one percent of voting-age blacks, about 250 people, were registered. They were kept from the polls, not by their own indifference or alienation but by systematic exclusion, by the poll tax, by intimidation, by literacy testing that even the testers, themselves, could not pass. And they were kept away from the polls by violence.

It must be hard for the young people in this audience to believe, but just 35 years ago, Americans, both black and white, lost their lives in the voting rights crusade. Some died in Selma and Marion. One of the reasons I came here

10 Thursday
Hallie Quinn Brown born 1850?

8AM

9

10

11

12

1PM

2

3

4

5

6

11 Friday
Ralph Abernathy born 1926

8AM

9

10

11

12

1PM

2

3

4

5

6

12 Saturday
SIGNING OF THE SOUTHERN MANIFESTO, A DOCUMENT PROTESTING THE BROWN VS. BOARD OF EDUCATION DECISION, 1956
Andrew Young born 1932

13 Sunday

today is to say to the families and those who remember—Jimmy Lee Jackson, Reverend James Reeb, Viola Liuzzo, and others whose names we may never know— we honor them for the patriots they were.

They did not die in vain. Just one week after Bloody Sunday, President Johnson spoke to the Nation in stirring words. He said, "At times, history and fate meet in a single time and a single place to shape a turning point in man's unending search for freedom. So it was at Lexington and Concord. So it was a century ago at Appomattox. So it was last week in Selma, Alabama. Their cause must be our cause."

Two weeks after Bloody Sunday, emboldened by their faith in God and the support of a white southerner in the Oval Office, Dr. King led 4,000 people across the Pettus Bridge on the 54-mile trek to Montgomery. And six months later, President Johnson signed the Voting Rights Act, proclaiming that the vote is the most powerful instrument ever devised for breaking down injustice and destroying the terrible walls which imprison men because they are different from other men. It has been said that the Voting Rights Act was signed in ink in Washington, but it first was signed in blood in Selma.

Those who walked by faith across this bridge led us all to a better tomorrow.
—President William J. Clinton

William J. Clinton, "Remarks on the 35th Anniversary of the 1965 Voting Rights March in Selma, Alabama," *Weekly Compilation of Presidential Documents* 36, no. 10 (2000), 471.

MARCH

S	M	T	W	T	F	S
		1	2	3	4	5
6	7	8	9	10	11	12
13	14	15	16	17	18	19
20	21	22	23	24	25	26
27	28	29	30	31		

APRIL

S	M	T	W	T	F	S
					1	2
3	4	5	6	7	8	9
10	11	12	13	14	15	16
17	18	19	20	21	22	23
24	25	26	27	28	29	30

MARCH 14-20

14 Monday
Fannie Lou Hamer dies 1977

8AM

9

10

11

12

1PM

2

3

4

5

6

15 Tuesday

8AM

9

10

11

12

1PM

2

3

4

5

6

16 Wednesday

8AM

9

10

11

12

1PM

2

3

4

5

6

"THE MYTHOLOGICAL PORTRAIT OF THE SOUTH"

Southern senators profoundly influenced the course of the civil rights struggle in America. Early in the twentieth-century battle for social equality, they settled on a policy of delay that had as its principal objective slowing what they perceived as an inexorable drive to destroy segregation. Their ability to stall civil rights advances in the United States Senate from the 1930s through the 1960s occurred because of their flexible tactics, along with their adoption of a more edifying argument in defense of segregation. The caucus could never have succeeded without the support of northern politicians, who utilized the constitutional arguments of southerners to validate their own lack of interest in Dixie's black citizens. In an article on the fight against anti-lynching legislation from 1920 through 1940, George Rable observed that southerners were caught completely off guard by the intensity of black protest in the 1950s and 1960s. Rable, however, overlooked the significance of the growing acceptance of strategic delay as an ordering mechanism for the southern fight in Washington. Irrational fears played no part in the construction of strategic delay as attested to by later civil rights developments that demonstrated the sound foundation on which southern senators staked their fight. They foresaw growing pressure against the region all along. These statesmen, however, misjudged the impact of legislative foot-dragging on the non-violent resistance

MARCH 2005

17 Thursday
ST. PATRICK'S DAY
Bayard Rustin born 1910
Myrlie Evers-Williams born 1933

8AM

9

10

11

12

1PM

2

3

4

5

6

18 Friday

8AM

9

10

11

12

1PM

2

3

4

5

6

19 Saturday

20 Sunday
PALM SUNDAY
VERNAL EQUINOX

movement. By preventing substantive civil rights advances through strategic delay and by failing to challenge the demagogues on the local level, southern senators unintentionally provided a catalyst for grass-roots activism. Once it became evident that Washington politicians would not act on civil rights legislation, black activists took the drive for social equality into the streets across the South. After a series of nonviolent protests culminated in violent white responses, northern legislators could no longer accept southern claims of the racial tranquility created by Jim Crow. Not until the extreme and widely reported turmoil surrounding the Birmingham civil rights protests in 1963 did many northern senators begin to seriously challenge the mythological portrait of the South described by southern senators. With southern prejudices exposed, the claims of the region's senators lost much of their credibility and, with that, the South lost segregation. The southern caucus had engaged in a successful rearguard battle for decades, but it could not outlast the impact of the grass-roots protest movement that its skillful delaying tactics helped to produce.

—Keith M. Finley

Keith M. Finley, "Southern Opposition to Civil Rights in the United States Senate: A Tactical and Ideological Analysis, 1938-1965" (Ph.D. dissertation, Louisiana State University, 2003), 16-18.

MARCH

S	M	T	W	T	F	S
		1	2	3	4	5
6	7	8	9	10	11	12
13	14	15	16	17	18	19
20	21	22	23	24	25	26
27	28	29	30	31		

APRIL

S	M	T	W	T	F	S
					1	2
3	4	5	6	7	8	9
10	11	12	13	14	15	16
17	18	19	20	21	22	23
24	25	26	27	28	29	30

21 Monday
SELMA-TO-MONTGOMERY
MARCH BEGINS, 1965

8AM

9

10

11

12

1PM

2

3

4

5

6

22 Tuesday

8AM

9

10

11

12

1PM

2

3

4

5

6

23 Wednesday

8AM

9

10

11

12

1PM

2

3

4

5

6

"MOST OF THE NATION WAS REPULSED"

Early in 1965, the SCLC [Southern Christian Leadership Council] brought its voter registration campaign to Selma, Alabama, a site chosen partly because of the presence there of a law enforcement officer of Bull Connor-like proclivities, Dallas County sheriff Jim Clark. The result was another resounding success. Clark's brutalization of nonresisting demonstrators culminated in Bloody Sunday, March 7, 1965, when law enforcement officers viciously assaulted marchers as they crossed the Edmund Pettus Bridge on the way to Montgomery. Governor [George] Wallace had promised that the march would be broken up by whatever measures were necessary, and his chief law enforcement lieutenant later insisted that the governor himself had given the order to attack. That evening, ABC television broadcast a lengthy film report of peaceful demonstrators being assailed by stampeding horses, flailing clubs, and tear gas. Most of the nation was repulsed. Over the following week, sympathy demonstrations took place

24 Thursday

25 Friday
GOOD FRIDAY

26 Saturday

8AM

9

10

11

12

1PM

2

3

4

5

6

8AM

9

10

11

12

1PM

2

3

4

5

6

27 Sunday
EASTER

across America. Citizens demanded remedial action from their congressional representatives, scores of whom condemned the violence and endorsed voting rights legislation. On March 15, 1965, President Johnson proposed such legislation before a joint session of Congress, as seventy million Americans watched on television.

The beating of peaceful black demonstrators by southern white law enforcement officers repulsed national opinion and led directly to the passage of landmark civil rights legislation.

—Michael J. Klarman

MARCH

S	M	T	W	T	F	S
		1	2	3	4	5
6	7	8	9	10	11	12
13	14	15	16	17	18	19
20	21	22	23	24	25	26
27	28	29	30	31		

APRIL

S	M	T	W	T	F	S
					1	2
3	4	5	6	7	8	9
10	11	12	13	14	15	16
17	18	19	20	21	22	23
24	25	26	27	28	29	30

Michael J. Klarman, "Race and Rights," in Christopher L. Tomlins and Michael Grossberg, *Cambridge History of Law in America, Volume 3, 1920-2000* (Cambridge: Cambridge University Press, 2004), 43.

28 Monday

8AM

9

10

11

12

1PM

2

3

4

5

6

29 Tuesday

8AM

9

10

11

12

1PM

2

3

4

5

6

30 Wednesday

8AM

9

10

11

12

1PM

2

3

4

5

6

"THE SIMPLE DIGNITY OF SITTING ON THOSE STOOLS"

In the spring of 1958, I started a new job without a car, which anchored me to the downtown area for lunch. I remember going to F. W. Woolworth one day for lunch and standing in line with other blacks behind a two-foot board at one end of a long lunch counter. Looking at the whites seated at the counter, some staring up at us, I suddenly felt the humiliation and shame that others must have felt many, many times in this unspoken dialogue about their power and our humanity. Excluded from the simple dignity of sitting on those stools, blacks had to take their lunch out in bags and eat elsewhere. Bringing lunch from home

thereafter was only quiet acquiescence to what I had faced in that line.

No flash of insight led me to confront this humiliation. It was, like other defining moments in that era, the growing political consciousness within the black community, born of discrete acts of oppression and resistance. That consciousness told me that my situation was not tolerable, that it was time at last to do something.

The Civil Rights Movement during the Eisenhower years, 1953 to 1961, was truly national—not merely in that it was an expression of African Americans, but also in its

31 Thursday

8AM

9

10

11

12

1PM

2

3

4

5

6

1 Friday

8AM

9

10

11

12

1PM

2

3

4

5

6

2 Saturday

3 Sunday

DAYLIGHT SAVING TIME BEGINS
John Willis Menard born 1838

geographical breadth. However, what have emerged in popular history as the origins of the movement are the Montgomery bus boycott in 1955 and '56, which propelled Martin Luther King Jr. into prominence, and the "first" sit-in in Greensboro, N.C., in 1960, which launched the Southern student movement and the Student Nonviolent Coordinating Committee.

This Southern interpretation of our history, due in part to our image of the South, underplays its national character. The South was always regarded by everyone—black and white, North and South—as the most dangerous territory in America for blacks: Look at the lynching of Emmett Till in Mississippi in 1955, at the violent resistance by white Southerners to school integration after 1955, at the events surrounding the desegregation of Central High School in Little Rock, Ark., in 1957 and '58.

—Ronald Walters

Ronald Walters, "Standing Up in America's Heartland," *American Visions* 8, no. 1 (1993), 20-24.

MARCH

S	M	T	W	T	F	S
		1	2	3	4	5
6	7	8	9	10	11	12
13	14	15	16	17	18	19
20	21	22	23	24	25	26
27	28	29	30	31		

APRIL

S	M	T	W	T	F	S
					1	2
3	4	5	6	7	8	9
10	11	12	13	14	15	16
17	18	19	20	21	22	23
24	25	26	27	28	29	30

4 Monday
Martin Luther King Jr. dies 1968

8AM

9

10

11

12

1PM

2

3

4

5

6

5 Tuesday
Robert Smalls born 1839
Booker T. Washington born 1856

8AM

9

10

11

12

1PM

2

3

4

5

6

6 Wednesday

8AM

9

10

11

12

1PM

2

3

4

5

6

"THE COMMON LANGUAGE OF WORK, SUFFERING, AND PROTEST"

I FEEL CLOSER TO MY COUNTRY THAN EVER. There is no longer a feeling of lonesome isolation. Instead—peace. I return without fearing prejudice that once bothered me . . . for I know that people practice cruel bigotry in their ignorance, not maliciously. . . .

I've learned that my people are not the only ones oppressed. . . . I have sung my songs all over the world and everywhere found that some common bond makes the people of all lands take to Negro songs as their own.

When I sang my American folk melodies in Budapest, Prague, Tiflis, Moscow, Oslo, or the Hebrides or on the Spanish front, the people understood and wept or rejoiced with the spirit of the songs. I found that where forces have been the same, whether people weave, build, pick cotton, or dig in the mine, they understand each other in the common language of work, suffering, and protest.

—Paul Robeson

7 Thursday

8 Friday

9 Saturday
Paul Robeson born 1898

8AM

9

10

11

12

1PM

2

3

4

5

6

8AM

9

10

11

12

1PM

2

3

4

5

6

10 Sunday

APRIL

S	M	T	W	T	F	S
					1	2
3	4	5	6	7	8	9
10	11	12	13	14	15	16
17	18	19	20	21	22	23
24	25	26	27	28	29	30

MAY

S	M	T	W	T	F	S
1	2	3	4	5	6	7
8	9	10	11	12	13	14
15	16	17	18	19	20	21
22	23	24	25	26	27	28
29	30	31				

Paul Robeson, New York interview, in Susan Robeson, *The Whole World in His Hands: Paul Robeson, a Family Memoir in Words and Pictures* (Secaucus, NJ: Carol Publishing Group, September 1981), 120.

11 Monday

12 Tuesday

Horace Roscoe Cayton Jr. born 1903

13 Wednesday

8AM	8AM	8AM
9	9	9
10	10	10
11	11	11
12	12	12
1PM	1PM	1PM
2	2	2
3	3	3
4	4	4
5	5	5
6	6	6

"JACKIE ROBINSON HAD TO BE BIGGER THAN LIFE"

They say certain people are bigger than life, but Jackie Robinson is the only man I've known who truly was. In 1947 life in America—at least my America, and Jackie's—was segregation. It was two worlds that were afraid of each other. There were separate schools for blacks and whites, separate restaurants, separate hotels, separate drinking fountains and separate baseball leagues. Life was unkind to black people who tried to bring those worlds together. It could be hateful. But Jackie Robinson, God bless him, was bigger than all of that.

Jackie Robinson had to be bigger than life. He had to be bigger than the Brooklyn teammates who got up a petition to keep him off the ball club, bigger than the pitchers who threw at him or the base runners who dug their spikes into his shin, bigger than the bench jockeys who hollered for him to carry their bags and shine their shoes, bigger than the so-called fans who mocked him with mops on their heads and wrote him death threats.

When Branch Rickey first met with Jackie about joining the Dodgers, he told him that for three years he would have

14 Thursday

8AM

9

10

11

12

1PM

2

3

4

5

6

15 Friday

JACKIE ROBINSON INTEGRATES BASEBALL, 1947
FORMATION OF STUDENT NONVIOLENT
COORDINATING COMMITTEE (SNCC), 1960
(THROUGH APRIL 17)

8AM

9

10

11

12

1PM

2

3

4

5

6

16 Saturday

17 Sunday

to turn the other cheek and silently suffer all the vile things that would come his way. Believe me, it wasn't Jackie's nature to do that. He was a fighter, the proudest and most competitive person I've ever seen. This was a man who, as a lieutenant in the Army, risked a court-martial by refusing to sit in the back of a military bus. But when Rickey read to him from *The Life of Christ*, Jackie understood the wisdom and the necessity of forbearance.

To this day, I don't know how he withstood the things he did without lashing back. I've been through a lot in my time, and I consider myself to be a patient man, but I know I couldn't have done what Jackie did. I don't think anybody else could have done it. Somehow, though, Jackie had the strength to suppress his instincts, to sacrifice his pride for his people's. It was an incredible act of selflessness that brought the races closer together than ever before and shaped the dreams of an entire generation.

—Hank Aaron remembering Jackie Robinson

Henry (Hank) Aaron, "Jackie Robinson," *Time* 153, no. 23 (1999), 104.

APRIL

S	M	T	W	T	F	S
					1	2
3	4	5	6	7	8	9
10	11	12	13	14	15	16
17	18	19	20	21	22	23
24	25	26	27	28	29	30

MAY

S	M	T	W	T	F	S
1	2	3	4	5	6	7
8	9	10	11	12	13	14
15	16	17	18	19	20	21
22	23	24	25	26	27	28
29	30	31				

18 Monday

8AM

9

10

11

12

1PM

2

3

4

5

6

19 Tuesday

8AM

9

10

11

12

1PM

2

3

4

5

6

20 Wednesday

8AM

9

10

11

12

1PM

2

3

4

5

6

"ARE YOU REALLY THE LAND OF THE FREE AND THE HOME OF THE BRAVE?"

It was an eye-opening experience to go into the deep south and to Mississippi and watch African Americans have to descend from the sidewalks as whites approached, and where blacks knew that it may mean death if they looked at white people in the eye. They dropped their heads or looked the other way as whites approached. It was an eerie experience. I shall never forget the dogs, fire hoses, armored tanks with machine guns, baseball bats, the beatings, the shots fired at us, the deaths—all to give African Americans the opportunity to freely exercise their rights under the Constitution of the United States.

I have spent my life never far from those days 40 years ago. I moved from marching and demonstrating to the avenue of social change by economic development and parity for African Americans. As I have said in speeches across the country a thousand times, "*America, are you really America to me? America, are you really the land of the free and the home of the brave?*"

Forty years ago, the answer to that question was no.

—Avon Rollins Sr., member of the Executive Committee of SNCC

21 Thursday

22 Friday

23 Saturday
PASSOVER BEGINS AT SUNDOWN

8AM

9

10

11

12

1PM

2

3

4

5

6

8AM

9

10

11

12

1PM

2

3

4

5

6

24 Sunday

Avon Rollins Sr., "SNCC, Tennessee, Virginia, North Carolina, Alabama, Mississippi,"
http://www.crmvet.org/vet/rollins.htm.

APRIL

S	M	T	W	T	F	S
					1	2
3	4	5	6	7	8	9
10	11	12	13	14	15	16
17	18	19	20	21	22	23
24	25	26	27	28	29	30

MAY

S	M	T	W	T	F	S
1	2	3	4	5	6	7
8	9	10	11	12	13	14
15	16	17	18	19	20	21
22	23	24	25	26	27	28
29	30	31				

25 Monday

8AM

9

10

11

12

1PM

2

3

4

5

6

26 Tuesday
FOUNDING OF MISSISSIPPI FREEDOM
DEMOCRATIC PARTY, 1964

8AM

9

10

11

12

1PM

2

3

4

5

6

27 Wednesday
Coretta Scott King born 1927

8AM

9

10

11

12

1PM

2

3

4

5

6

A REAL PARTY ✳✳✳✳✳✳ ✳✳✳✳✳✳ OF THE PEOPLE

When Mississippi blacks led by Fannie Lou Hamer crashed the Democratic Convention in 1964, they rocked the party to its foundations, challenging the segregationist state delegation, upsetting their own leaders, and infuriating the President of the United States. But they were heard.

The Mississippi Freedom Democratic Party was born in Jackson's black Masonic temple on April 26, 1964, when the fewer than 300 people on hand seemed swallowed up by the hall's vastness. Such a pitiful turnout revealed the utter absurdity of such a venture, the party's many critics declared. Even more ridiculous was the party's plan to run black candidates for Congress in June's Democratic primary, and then send a delegation to the Democratic National Convention in August, to call into question the regular Mississippi delegates' right to be seated. The whole thing was nothing but a pipe dream. How could Mississippi blacks, most of whom weren't even allowed to vote, hope to pose any sort of threat to the state's white political establishment?

But that was not the way the party's founders viewed their creation. They saw themselves as a bulwark of true democracy, a real party of the people of Mississippi, open to both blacks and whites. Moreover, women, who had been in the forefront of the civil rights struggle, would now play integral roles in the MFDP, at a time when in most state

28 Thursday

8AM

9

10

11

12

1PM

2

3

4

5

6

29 Friday

8AM

9

10

11

12

1PM

2

3

4

5

6

30 Saturday

1 Sunday

party organizations, Democratic or Republican, women had little voice or influence, even though they did much, if not most, of the day-to-day work. Fannie Lou Hamer, a dogged leader in the drive, in previous years, to register Mississippi blacks to vote, was at the center of the new party, along with Victoria Gray, Annie Devine, and numerous other women. There were so many of them, in fact, that Lawrence Guyot, the chairman of the MFDP, at one point told Hamer, Gray, and Devine that it was time for the women to step back and allow men to come forward. It didn't take him long to disavow that statement. "I came to the movement a chauvinist and a fool, and I got thoroughly educated very, very quickly," he said.

—Lynne Olson

Lynne Olson, "We Didn't Come All This Way for No Two Seats," *American Legacy: Celebrating African-American History & Culture* 7, no. 1 (2001), 55.

APRIL

S	M	T	W	T	F	S
					1	2
3	4	5	6	7	8	9
10	11	12	13	14	15	16
17	18	19	20	21	22	23
24	25	26	27	28	29	30

MAY

S	M	T	W	T	F	S
1	2	3	4	5	6	7
8	9	10	11	12	13	14
15	16	17	18	19	20	21
22	23	24	25	26	27	28
29	30	31				

2 Monday

8AM

9

10

11

12

1PM

2

3

4

5

6

3 Tuesday

8AM

9

10

11

12

1PM

2

3

4

5

6

4 Wednesday

8AM

9

10

11

12

1PM

2

3

4

5

6

"THEIR VERSION OF SOUTHERN HOSPITALITY"

After their departure from Washington, D.C., the Freedom Riders encountered little difficulty until they reached Alabama. On May 14, 1961, the two buses, about an hour apart, headed for Anniston, Alabama, with a planned stop for the night in Birmingham. The Greyhound bus arrived in Anniston first, with the Riders and two undercover Alabama state investigators on board. A mob, warned of the arrival, attacked the bus at the station, trying to drag the Riders out onto the platform. The Alabama policemen, dropping their guise, urged the driver to leave. The tires of the bus were slashed, however, and it ground to a halt outside of Anniston. The mob caught up, threw a firebomb into the bus, and forced its occupants out to endure their version of southern hospitality. The second bus was also attacked in Anniston, but escaped to the dubious refuge of Birmingham.

After reaching Birmingham, the Riders emerged to confront a crowd armed with "baseball bats, lead pipes, and bicycle chains." The Riders were beaten so badly that an FBI agent, carefully watching and recording the scene, said that he "couldn't see their faces through the blood."

—John M. Murphy

5 Thursday

8AM

9

10

11

12

1PM

2

3

4

5

6

6 Friday

8AM

9

10

11

12

1PM

2

3

4

5

6

7 Saturday

8 Sunday
MOTHER'S DAY

MAY

S	M	T	W	T	F	S
1	2	3	4	5	6	7
8	9	10	11	12	13	14
15	16	17	18	19	20	21
22	23	24	25	26	27	28
29	30	31				

JUNE

S	M	T	W	T	F	S
				1	2	3	4
5	6	7	8	9	10	11
12	13	14	15	16	17	18
19	20	21	22	23	24	25
26	27	28	29	30		

John M. Murphy, "Domesticating Dissent: The Kennedys and the Freedom Rides," *Communication Monographs* 92, no. 1 (1992), 61-79.

9 Monday

8AM

9

10

11

12

1PM

2

3

4

5

6

10 Tuesday

8AM

9

10

11

12

1PM

2

3

4

5

6

11 Wednesday

8AM

9

10

11

12

1PM

2

3

4

5

6

AN ACT OF SIMPLE KINDNESS

May 14, 1961, Mother's Day—A Greyhound bus carrying the first of the Freedom Riders was attacked by an armed mob at the terminal in Anniston, Alabama. The mob slashed the tires and chased the bus a few miles down the highway toward Birmingham, until the flattening tires forced the driver to pull off the road in front of Forsyth's country store. Windows were smashed, a firebomb tossed inside and the bus went up in flames; as the riders tumbled out they were beaten by the waiting mob. But, from the same incident, a different memory. Against the background of violence and hatred, a twelve-year-old white girl—seeing the victims of the mob, some wounded, all thirsty—carried drinking water from her nearby home to relieve their distress. It was an act of simple kindness that earned her the scorn of her peers all during her adolescent years. At eighteen she left Anniston for college, and never returned.

—William B. Cooper

12 Thursday

8AM

9

10

11

12

1PM

2

3

4

5

6

13 Friday

8AM

9

10

11

12

1PM

2

3

4

5

6

14 Saturday

15 Sunday

Alvin Poussaint born 1954

MAY

S	M	T	W	T	F	S
1	2	3	4	5	6	7
8	9	10	11	12	13	14
15	16	17	18	19	20	21
22	23	24	25	26	27	28
29	30	31				

JUNE

S	M	T	W	T	F	S
			1	2	3	4
5	6	7	8	9	10	11
12	13	14	15	16	17	18
19	20	21	22	23	24	25
26	27	28	29	30		

William B. Cooper, "They Had a Dream," *Commonweal* 119, no. 14 (1992), 13-14.

16 Monday

8AM

9

10

11

12

1PM

2

3

4

5

6

17 Tuesday

8AM

9

10

11

12

1PM

2

3

4

5

6

18 Wednesday

Mary McLeod Bethune dies 1955

8AM

9

10

11

12

1PM

2

3

4

5

6

"MALCOLM WAS OUR MANHOOD"

And if you knew him you would know why we must honor him.

Malcolm was our manhood, our living, black manhood! This was his meaning to his people. And, in honoring him, we honor the best in ourselves. Last year, from Africa, he wrote these words to a friend: "My journey," he says, "is almost ended, and I have a much broader scope than when I started out, which I believe will add new life and dimension to our struggle for freedom and honor and dignity in the States. I am writing these things so that you will know for a fact the tremendous sympathy and support we have among the African States for our Human Rights struggle. The main thing is that we keep a United Front wherein our most valuable time and energy will not be wasted fighting each other." However we may have differed with him—or with each other about him and his value as a man—let his going from us serve only to bring us together, now.

Consigning these mortal remains to earth, the

19 Thursday
Malcolm X born 1925

8AM

9

10

11

12

1PM

2

3

4

5

6

20 Friday

8AM

9

10

11

12

1PM

2

3

4

5

6

21 Saturday

22 Sunday

common mother of all, secure in the knowledge that what we place in the ground is no more now a man—but a seed—which, after the winter of our discontent, will come forth again to meet us. And we will know him then for what he was and is—a Prince—our own black shining Prince!—who didn't hesitate to die, because he loved us so.

—Ossie Davis, Malcolm X's Eulogy Delivered at the Faith Temple Church of God, February 27, 1965.

MAY

S	M	T	W	T	F	S
1	2	3	4	5	6	7
8	9	10	11	12	13	14
15	16	17	18	19	20	21
22	23	24	25	26	27	28
29	30	31				

JUNE

S	M	T	W	T	F	S
			1	2	3	4
5	6	7	8	9	10	11
12	13	14	15	16	17	18
19	20	21	22	23	24	25
26	27	28	29	30		

The Official Malcolm X Website, http://www.cmgww.com/historic/malcolm/about/eulogy.htm

23 Monday

8AM

9

10

11

12

1PM

2

3

4

5

6

24 Tuesday

8AM

9

10

11

12

1PM

2

3

4

5

6

25 Wednesday

8AM

9

10

11

12

1PM

2

3

4

5

6

THE BASIC FUNCTION OF ARMED RESISTANCE

The civil rights movement of the 1950s and 1960s in the American South is often characterized as a nonviolent revolution. Scholarly and popular literature and media re-creations of the movement rarely emphasize the significance of armed resistance in the struggle of black people for desegregation, political and economic rights, and basic human dignity. In dozens of Southern communities, black people picked up arms to defend their lives, property and battle for human rights. Black people relied on armed self-defense, particularly in communities where federal government officials failed to protect movement activists and supporters from the violence of racists and segregationists, who were often supported by local law enforcement. Armed resistance played a significant role in allowing black communities and the movement to survive and continue. The Mississippi Freedom Summer campaign and the drive for political and human rights in McComb, Mississippi, in 1964 illustrate well the dynamic role played by armed resistance in the Southern freedom movement.

—Akinyele O. Umoja

26 Thursday

8AM

9

10

11

12

1PM

2

3

4

5

6

27 Friday

8AM

9

10

11

12

1PM

2

3

4

5

6

28 Saturday

29 Sunday

Akinyele O. Umoja, "1964: The Beginning of the End of Nonviolence in the Mississippi Freedom Movement," *Radical History Review* 85 (2003), 201.

MAY

S	M	T	W	T	F	S
1	2	3	4	5	6	7
8	9	10	11	12	13	14
15	16	17	18	19	20	21
22	23	24	25	26	27	28
29	30	31				

JUNE

S	M	T	W	T	F	S
			1	2	3	4
5	6	7	8	9	10	11
12	13	14	15	16	17	18
19	20	21	22	23	24	25
26	27	28	29	30		

30 Monday
MEMORIAL DAY OBSERVED
James Earl Chaney born 1943

8AM

9

10

11

12

1PM

2

3

4

5

6

31 Tuesday
U.S. SUPREME COURT ORDERS LOWER COURTS
TO USE "ALL DELIBERATE SPEED" IN
DESEGREGATING PUBLIC SCHOOLS IN
BROWN II, 1955

8AM

9

10

11

12

1PM

2

3

4

5

6

1 Wednesday

8AM

9

10

11

12

1PM

2

3

4

5

6

A SOCIAL REVOLUTION

I was a part of the civil rights movement, involved in spectacular legal victories which we are not going to duplicate in this century. In the next century, there may be some other movement equally spectacular in terms of legal decisions, but the Supreme Court decisions of 1954 to '64 are exceptional in terms of their constitutional significance. In one case after the other, segregation was stricken as unconstitutional. This resulted in a revolution in this country—a social revolution.

Birmingham in 1954 and '55, that was a scary place. Now it has emerged and they have a black mayor. I never thought I would live long enough to see that much change.

—Constance Baker Motley

2 Thursday
Cornel West born 1953

8AM

9

10

11

12

1PM

2

3

4

5

6

3 Friday

8AM

9

10

11

12

1PM

2

3

4

5

6

4 Saturday

5 Sunday

MAY

S	M	T	W	T	F	S
1	2	3	4	5	6	7
8	9	10	11	12	13	14
15	16	17	18	19	20	21
22	23	24	25	26	27	28
29	30	31				

JUNE

S	M	T	W	T	F	S
			1	2	3	4
5	6	7	8	9	10	11
12	13	14	15	16	17	18
19	20	21	22	23	24	25
26	27	28	29	30		

Constance Baker Motley, in Brian Lanker, *I Dream A World: Portraits of Black Women Who Changed America* (New York: Stewart, Tabori & Chang, 1989), 65.

6 Monday

8AM

9

10

11

12

1PM

2

3

4

5

6

7 Tuesday

8AM

9

10

11

12

1PM

2

3

4

5

6

8 Wednesday

8AM

9

10

11

12

1PM

2

3

4

5

6

"MISSISSIPPI HAD SENT A MESSAGE TO THE WORLD THAT IT WAS ALL RIGHT TO KILL A BLACK MAN"

[H]E WAS THE VOICE OF CIVIL RIGHTS IN OUR STATE. He investigated murders and lynchings, planned voter registration drives, organized boycotts, and fought to gain access for our people and representation where there was none. Because of such efforts, many die-hard segregationists believed Medgar's voice had to be silenced. Byron De La Beckwith took it upon himself to see that it was.

Twice before, the evidence against Beckwith had been heard, but each trial ended with a hung jury. Both times, twelve men—all of them White—could not agree on a verdict, and Beckwith was set free. Twice before, in the case of Medgar's murder, and in countless other instances as well, Mississippi had sent a message to the world that it was all right to kill a Black man. In my view, Byron De La Beckwith wasn't the only one on trial. So was Mississippi.

—Myrlie Evers-Williams

JUNE 2005

9 Thursday

8AM

9

10

11

12

1PM

2

3

4

5

6

10 Friday

8AM

9

10

11

12

1PM

2

3

4

5

6

11 Saturday

12 Sunday

MEDGAR EVERS ASSASSINATED, 1963

Myrlie Evers-Williams and Melinda Blau, *Watch Me Fly: What I Learned on the Way to Becoming the Woman I Was Meant to Be* (New York: Little, Brown & Company), 1999.

JUNE

S	M	T	W	T	F	S
			1	2	3	4
5	6	7	8	9	10	11
12	13	14	15	16	17	18
19	20	21	22	23	24	25
26	27	28	29	30		

JULY

S	M	T	W	T	F	S
					1	2
3	4	5	6	7	8	9
10	11	12	13	14	15	16
17	18	19	20	21	22	23
24/31	25	26	27	28	29	30

13 Monday

14 Tuesday
FLAG DAY

15 Wednesday

8AM	8AM	8AM
9	9	9
10	10	10
11	11	11
12	12	12
1PM	1PM	1PM
2	2	2
3	3	3
4	4	4
5	5	5
6	6	6

✳ JUNETEENTH ✳

Everybody involved in the Civil Rights Movement shared the same immediate goals: the outlawing of legal racial segregation, and the guaranteeing of black voting, civil liberties, and equality under the law. Beyond these clear goals, there were tremendous ideological and political differences between groups and individuals. Some people hated each other almost as much as they opposed the white racists. But the successful construction of a united front requires unity without uniformity. There will be a need for divergent personalities and organizations to build a broad, popular movement.

Historians frequently make the mistake of telling a story from the vantage point of "great" people's (usually men's) lives. To be sure, an unusual number of talented and extraordinary black women and men came into the public arena a generation ago, to push forward measures to outlaw American apartheid. . . .

Creative and talented individuals often help to define a moment in history, yet history is fundamentally made by ordinary people, who work every day, who sacrifice for their children, and find social meaning through their struggles and contributions to their communities, voluntary organizations, and religious institutions. The struggle for freedom was always expressed in collective terms for the African-American people. The spirit of freedom was expressed in their celebrations of what was first termed "Negro History Month" held every February; through celebrations such as "Juneteenth," honoring the date of

16 Thursday

8AM

9

10

11

12

1PM

2

3

4

5

6

17 Friday

8AM

9

10

11

12

1PM

2

3

4

5

6

18 Saturday

19 Sunday

FATHER'S DAY
JUNETEENTH

June 19, 1865, when blacks in Texas first learned of their emancipation from slavery. . . . Black people regardless of their social class deeply felt a sense of linked fates, which bound them to each other, as well as to their collective history of resistance. The successes of any one member of a disadvantaged community are, in many ways, shared and experienced by all.

The modern desegregation movement was successfully constructed, and was able to transform America's political and social institutions, because it fully reflected that national black consciousness, a collective identity born of triumphs as well as tragedies, the fruit of deferred dreams and democratic aspirations.

—Manning Marable

Manning Marable, "Reparations, Black Consciousness, and the Black Freedom Struggle," http://www.freepress.org/columns/display/4/2002/488.

JUNE

S	M	T	W	T	F	S
			1	2	3	4
5	6	7	8	9	10	11
12	13	14	15	16	17	18
19	20	21	22	23	24	25
26	27	28	29	30		

JULY

S	M	T	W	T	F	S
					1	2
3	4	5	6	7	8	9
10	11	12	13	14	15	16
17	18	19	20	21	22	23
24/31	25	26	27	28	29	30

20 Monday

8AM

9

10

11

12

1PM

2

3

4

5

6

21 Tuesday

SUMMER SOLSTICE
Joseph Hayne Rainey born 1832

8AM

9

10

11

12

1PM

2

3

4

5

6

22 Wednesday

8AM

9

10

11

12

1PM

2

3

4

5

6

ONLY TWENTY-EIGHT MILES

THREE AND A HALF YEARS AFTER FIVE THOUSAND FEDERAL troops had stood guard as he became the first black student at the University of Mississippi, James Meredith on June 5 [1966] began a one-man march to encourage black voter registration in the Deep South. He made a conspicuous figure setting out from Memphis, Tennessee, with a carved African walking stick and yellow pith helmet. The trek he planned would take him through two hundred-odd miles of rural Mississippi, past Oxford, where he had attended Ole Miss, past his native Kosciusko, and on to Jackson. Some 450,000 eligible black voters were unregistered in the state, said Meredith, and "if I can do it, maybe they can, too."

On his second day out, as he made his way along U.S. Highway 51, an ambusher near Hernando, Mississippi, shot Meredith in the back. He had walked only twenty-eight miles. The initial Associated Press report pronounced him dead at 6:33 P.M. Radio and television programming across the country was interrupted to give the news of his death. In fact, his wounds were not critical; seventy shotgun pellets scattered across his shoulders, neck, and legs were removed at a nearby hospital. Aubrey James Norvell, an unemployed hardware contractor, confessed to the shooting but was unable to tell police why he had done it.

Civil rights workers continued the march without Meredith until June 26, when he joined them for the final leg of the walk. A crowd of twelve thousand rallied at Jackson to mark the journey's end.

—Nathan Ward

23 Thursday

8AM

9

10

11

12

1PM

2

3

4

5

6

24 Friday

8AM

9

10

11

12

1PM

2

3

4

5

6

25 Saturday

26 Sunday

Nathan Ward, "1966: Twenty-Five Years Ago," *American Heritage* 42, no. 3 (1991), 42-43.

JUNE

S	M	T	W	T	F	S
			1	2	3	4
5	6	7	8	9	10	11
12	13	14	15	16	17	18
19	20	21	22	23	24	25
26	27	28	29	30		

JULY

S	M	T	W	T	F	S
					1	2
3	4	5	6	7	8	9
10	11	12	13	14	15	16
17	18	19	20	21	22	23
24/31	25	26	27	28	29	30

27 Monday
M. Carl Holman born 1919

8AM

9

10

11

12

1PM

2

3

4

5

6

28 Tuesday

8AM

9

10

11

12

1PM

2

3

4

5

6

29 Wednesday
Stokely Carmichael born 1941

8AM

9

10

11

12

1PM

2

3

4

5

6

"IT CHEAPENED THE WORTH OF OUR COLLEGE DEGREES"

Like many others of my time and place, I was attracted to the 1960 sit-ins against segregated lunch counters because they offered me, at age 20, an opportunity to directly confront and attack an evil system which kept me away not only from an integrated cup of coffee but also from the jobs that even my Morehouse College degree wouldn't have qualified me for.

I would never have the major qualification for many ordinary jobs—dime-store clerk, bank teller, policeman who could arrest White people. The prerequisite for these jobs was a White skin, and the assault on lunch counters was an assault on the barriers that prevented me and thousands of young people like me from realizing our potential.

Segregation and racism frustrated our ever achieving the futures we had trained for; it cheapened the worth of our college degrees. And it crippled the lives of every Black person—college students and first grade dropouts. So we sat-in and rode-in and marched and protested—but we also did much more.

We organized. We spent long hours convincing others to

30 Thursday

8AM

9

10

11

12

1PM

2

3

4

5

6

1 Friday
CANADA DAY

8AM

9

10

11

12

1PM

2

3

4

5

6

2 Saturday
LYNDON JOHNSON SIGNS
CIVIL RIGHTS ACT, 1964
Thurgood Marshall born 1908
Medgar Evers born 1925

3 Sunday

make a dangerous attempt to register to vote. To become a member of a brand-new political party. To join a labor union. To take steps that would help improve their lives. To join with others in a struggle that had begun long before we had been born and which we hoped would continue after we had left the scene.

By the mid-sixties, we had won some fights. Legal segregation was eliminated by the Civil Rights Act of 1964. Discrimination at the ballot box was voted out by the Voting Rights Act of 1965.

—Julian Bond, Chairman of the Board, NAACP

JUNE

S	M	T	W	T	F	S
			1	2	3	4
5	6	7	8	9	10	11
12	13	14	15	16	17	18
19	20	21	22	23	24	25
26	27	28	29	30		

JULY

S	M	T	W	T	F	S
					1	2
3	4	5	6	7	8	9
10	11	12	13	14	15	16
17	18	19	20	21	22	23
24/31	25	26	27	28	29	30

Julian Bond, "Passing the Torch?" *Black Collegian*, April 1996, 41.

4 Monday
INDEPENDENCE DAY

8AM

9

10

11

12

1PM

2

3

4

5

6

5 Tuesday

8AM

9

10

11

12

1PM

2

3

4

5

6

6 Wednesday

8AM

9

10

11

12

1PM

2

3

4

5

6

"I LEAVE YOU FINALLY A RESPONSIBILITY TO OUR YOUNG PEOPLE"

The world around us really belongs to youth for youth will take over its future management. Our children must never lose their zeal for building a better world. They must not be discouraged from aspiring toward greatness, for they are to be the leaders of tomorrow. Nor must they forget that the masses of our people are still underprivileged, ill-housed, impoverished and victimized by discrimination. We have a powerful potential in our youth, and we must have the courage to change old ideas and practices so that we may direct their power toward good ends.

Faith, courage, brotherhood, dignity, ambition, responsibility—these are needed today as never before.

We must cultivate them and use them as tools for our task of completing the establishment of equality for the Negro. We must sharpen these tools in the struggle that faces us and find new ways of using them. The Freedom Gates are half-ajar. We must pry them fully open.

If I have a legacy to leave my people, it is my philosophy of living and serving. As I face tomorrow, I am content, for I think I have spent my life well. I pray now that my philosophy may be helpful to those who share my vision of a world of Peace, Progress, Brotherhood, and Love.

—Mary McLeod Bethune

7 Thursday

8AM

9

10

11

12

1PM

2

3

4

5

6

8 Friday

8AM

9

10

11

12

1PM

2

3

4

5

6

9 Saturday

10 Sunday

Mary McLeod Bethune born 1875

JULY						
S	M	T	W	T	F	S
					1	2
3	4	5	6	7	8	9
10	11	12	13	14	15	16
17	18	19	20	21	22	23
24/31	25	26	27	28	29	30

AUGUST						
S	M	T	W	T	F	S
	1	2	3	4	5	6
7	8	9	10	11	12	13
14	15	16	17	18	19	20
21	22	23	24	25	26	27
28	29	30	31			

Mary McLeod Bethune, "My Last Will and Testament," *Ebony*, August 1955.

11 Monday

8AM

9

10

11

12

1PM

2

3

4

5

6

12 Tuesday

8AM

9

10

11

12

1PM

2

3

4

5

6

13 Wednesday

8AM

9

10

11

12

1PM

2

3

4

5

6

THE INEVITABLE IRONY OF A SOCIETY MORE JUST THAN THEIR OWN

The recent Civil Rights act exemplifies the formation of an idea expanded far beyond what the forefathers intended when they say "all men are created equal." Perhaps if the framers of 1776 had not declared the concept of equality in such universal terms it may have been more difficult to challenge and partially eradicate the pervasive barriers of discrimination on race and sex. But once the drafters and signers of our Declaration made the decision not to weaken their moral argument for nationhood by attempting to rationalize the lie many of them were living, they made inevitable the irony that the truth they espoused, and not their example, would eventually guide their progeny to a society more just than their own.

—A. Leon Higginbotham

14 Thursday

15 Friday

16 Saturday
Ida Bell Wells-Barnett born 1862

8AM	8AM
9	9
10	10
11	11
12	12
1PM	1PM
2	2
3	3
4	4
5	5
6	6

17 Sunday

JULY

S	M	T	W	T	F	S
					1	2
3	4	5	6	7	8	9
10	11	12	13	14	15	16
17	18	19	20	21	22	23
24/31	25	26	27	28	29	30

AUGUST

S	M	T	W	T	F	S
	1	2	3	4	5	6
7	8	9	10	11	12	13
14	15	16	17	18	19	20
21	22	23	24	25	26	27
28	29	30	31			

A. Leon Higginbotham, *In the Matter of Color: Race and the American Legal Process: The Colonial Period* (New York: Oxford University Press, 1978), 389.

18 Monday

8AM

9

10

11

12

1PM

2

3

4

5

6

19 Tuesday

8AM

9

10

11

12

1PM

2

3

4

5

6

20 Wednesday

8AM

9

10

11

12

1PM

2

3

4

5

6

"WE DIE STANDING ON OUR FEET FIGHTING"

[A. PHILIP] RANDOLPH'S REAL ACHIEVEMENT WAS THAT, as a low-status, black minority-group leader whose following largely lacked the resources of education, financial security, and influence in the dominant white community, he nevertheless devised a technique enabling blacks to make demands on the established decision makers. Randolph was undoubtedly the most creative black leader of the time; realizing that changed conditions called for novel strategies if blacks were to gain more political power and economic equality, he endeavored to supply those strategies so that the black community might benefit from the expanding wartime economy. Prior to his march threat, the white power structure had been unwilling to reallocate the resources of the larger community to help Afro-Americans. After Randolph's rise to prominence, freedom from oppression would no longer be sufficient; from then on, blacks would demand their proportionate share of the nation's economic wealth. Never again would the Afro-American minority be content to beg for favors from white patrons. "Rather we die standing on our feet fighting for our rights than to exist upon our knees begging for life," Randolph proclaimed.

—Paula F. Pfeffer

21 Thursday

SIGNING OF EXECUTIVE ORDER 9981, ENDING
SEGREGATION IN THE U.S. ARMED FORCES,
DUE TO PRESSURE ORGANIZED BY
A. PHILIP RANDOLPH, 1948

8AM

9

10

11

12

1PM

2

3

4

5

6

22 Friday

8AM

9

10

11

12

1PM

2

3

4

5

6

23 Saturday

24 Sunday

Charles Spurgeon Johnson born 1893
Kenneth Bancroft Clark born 1914

			JULY			
S	M	T	W	T	F	S
					1	2
3	4	5	6	7	8	9
10	11	12	13	14	15	16
17	18	19	20	21	22	23
24/31	25	26	27	28	29	30

			AUGUST			
S	M	T	W	T	F	S
	1	2	3	4	5	6
7	8	9	10	11	12	13
14	15	16	17	18	19	20
21	22	23	24	25	26	27
28	29	30	31			

Paula F. Pfeffer, *A. Philip Randolph, Pioneer of the Civil Rights Movement* (Baton Rouge: Louisiana State University Press, 1990), 300.

25 Monday

8AM

9

10

11

12

1PM

2

3

4

5

6

26 Tuesday

8AM

9

10

11

12

1PM

2

3

4

5

6

27 Wednesday

8AM

9

10

11

12

1PM

2

3

4

5

6

MORE THAN A UNION, MORE THAN A BROTHERHOOD

They were more than a union; they were, as their name aptly says, the Brotherhood of Sleeping Car Porters.

Forced to the bottom of the economic rung by racism and forced to perform routine work for tips and piddling wages, they turned the tables on their traducers, making a thing of awesome dignity out of their jobs and climbing, one writer said, "a ladder of yes-sirs," to the heights.

After a bitter 12-year struggle, during which hundreds were fired and repeated attempts were made to crush them, they triumphed and became on August 25, 1937, the first Black union to sign a contract with a major corporation. During these years and afterwards, especially in the pivotal '40s, the Brotherhood of Sleeping Car Porters became not only an economic force but a major arm of the Freedom Movement, making their pioneering president, Asa Philip Randolph, a preeminent leader of the African-American struggle.

It was from Randolph and the Brotherhood that the March on Washington idea came; it was Randolph and the Brotherhood who forced the Fair Employment Practices (FEPC) idea.

But they were bigger than one man. They were the united voices and strengths of 10,000 extraordinary ordinary men who taught us the dignity of work and the power of united workers.

—"Brotherhood of Sleeping Car Porters Honored," *Ebony*, February 2002, 84-85.

28 Thursday

8AM

9

10

11

12

1PM

2

3

4

5

6

29 Friday

8AM

9

10

11

12

1PM

2

3

4

5

6

30 Saturday

Elizabeth Ross Haynes born 1883

31 Sunday

Whitney M. Young Jr. born 1921

JULY

S	M	T	W	T	F	S
					1	2
3	4	5	6	7	8	9
10	11	12	13	14	15	16
17	18	19	20	21	22	23
24/31	25	26	27	28	29	30

AUGUST

S	M	T	W	T	F	S
	1	2	3	4	5	6
7	8	9	10	11	12	13
14	15	16	17	18	19	20
21	22	23	24	25	26	27
28	29	30	31			

1 Monday

8AM

9

10

11

12

1PM

2

3

4

5

6

2 Tuesday

8AM

9

10

11

12

1PM

2

3

4

5

6

3 Wednesday

8AM

9

10

11

12

1PM

2

3

4

5

6

YEARS OF EXCRUCIATING RISK

[I]t is hard to imagine masses of people lining up for years of excruciating risk against Southern sheriffs, fire hoses, and attack dogs without some transcendent or millennial faith to sustain them. It is hard to imagine such faith being sustained without emotional, mass rituals—without something extreme and extraordinary to link the masses' spirits together . . . it is impossible to ignore how often the participants carried their movement out in prophetic, ecstatic Biblical tones.

—David L. Chappell

4 Thursday

5 Friday

6 Saturday

LYNDON JOHNSON PASSES THE VOTING
RIGHTS ACT, WHICH MADE LITERACY
TESTS ILLEGAL, 1965

8AM
9
10
11
12
1PM
2
3
4
5
6

8AM
9
10
11
12
1PM
2
3
4
5
6

7 Sunday

Ralph Bunche born 1904

AUGUST

S	M	T	W	T	F	S
	1	2	3	4	5	6
7	8	9	10	11	12	13
14	15	16	17	18	19	20
21	22	23	24	25	26	27
28	29	30	31			

SEPTEMBER

S	M	T	W	T	F	S
				1	2	3
4	5	6	7	8	9	10
11	12	13	14	15	16	17
18	19	20	21	22	23	24
25	26	27	28	29	30	

David L. Chappell, "Religious Revivalism in the Civil Rights Movement," *African American Review* 36, no. 4 (2002), 581-596.

8 Monday

8AM

9

10

11

12

1PM

2

3

4

5

6

9 Tuesday

8AM

9

10

11

12

1PM

2

3

4

5

6

10 Wednesday

8AM

9

10

11

12

1PM

2

3

4

5

6

THE MOTHER OF ALL URBAN UPRISINGS

YES, IT WAS THE BLACK PEOPLE OF WATTS—JUST AS those in subsequent major '60s riots in Newark, Detroit, Philadelphia, Chicago, Cleveland and Washington—who suffered the most. It was our young men who were shot and killed by police, our neighborhoods that were patrolled by army tanks (a chilling sight I witnessed in Cleveland and will never forget) and our neighborhoods that burned.

But if Watts had not happened, chances are that Blacks would have continued being misused by the overbearing white power structure in general and individual whites in particular. The sound and fury of Watts served notice to the nation that Blacks no longer were willing to turn the other cheek to race-based indignities and harassment. It was time to stand up and be counted.

There's no question that Watts was a social revolution—a clear manifestation of an oppressed people tired of being called "nigger" by white police while being brutalized. Tired of downtrodden living conditions. Tired of being last hired and first fired. Tired.

After Watts, our country never would be the same.

Of course, many people, including, I suspect, most whites, will never understand how anyone could be driven to such high-risk acts of desperation, no matter the circumstances. How anyone could feel they were so bad off. How any single event or series of events could trigger such self-destructive civil and criminal disobedience.

11 Thursday

WATTS RIOTS BEGIN, 1965
Anna Julia Cooper born 1858

8AM

9

10

11

12

1PM

2

3

4

5

6

12 Friday

8AM

9

10

11

12

1PM

2

3

4

5

6

13 Saturday

14 Sunday

Although it seems irresponsible for any right-thinking individual, Black or white, to condone rioting in the streets, it is at least understandable as a tactic to protest discriminatory practices that serve to subjugate and degrade human beings. Think about it.

Unless you have tasted the bitter fruit of racial discrimination, you simply cannot comprehend the depth of despair it causes. Unless you have been denied employment because of your race or access to certain organizations or establishments or have been mistaken for the hired help at a social function, you simply cannot grasp the throbbing pain that grabs you in the gut.

Unless you have been treated shabbily by a department store clerk or openly followed by a security guard while browsing through a big discount drugstore or denied the opportunity to live where you want to live, you simply don't know the heart-wrenching, mind-sapping depression that envelops you like a shroud.

—Richard G. Carter

Richard G. Carter, "Recalling Watts: The Mother of All Urban Uprisings," *New York Amsterdam News* 89, no. 34 (1998), 18.

AUGUST

S	M	T	W	T	F	S
	1	2	3	4	5	6
7	8	9	10	11	12	13
14	15	16	17	18	19	20
21	22	23	24	25	26	27
28	29	30	31			

SEPTEMBER

S	M	T	W	T	F	S
				1	2	3
4	5	6	7	8	9	10
11	12	13	14	15	16	17
18	19	20	21	22	23	24
25	26	27	28	29	30	

AUGUST 15-21

15 Monday

16 Tuesday
Wyatt Tee Walker born 1929

17 Wednesday

8AM

9

10

11

12

1PM

2

3

4

5

6

"IN THE BASEMENT OF THE GREAT SOCIETY"

With all the struggle and all the achievements, we must face the fact, however, that the Negro still lives in the basement of the Great Society. He is still at the bottom, despite the few who have penetrated to slightly higher levels. Even where the door has been forced partially open, mobility for the Negro is still sharply restricted. There is often no bottom at which to start, and when there is there's almost no room at the top. In consequence, Negroes are still impoverished aliens in an affluent society. They are too poor even to rise with the society, too impoverished by the ages to be able to ascend by using their own resources. And the Negro did not do this himself; it was done to him. For more than half of his American history, he was enslaved. Yet, he built the spanning bridges and the grand mansions, the sturdy docks and stout factories of the South. His unpaid labor made cotton "King" and established America as a significant nation in international commerce. Even after his release from chattel slavery, the nation grew over him, submerging him. It became the richest, most powerful society in the history of man, but it left the Negro far behind.

—Martin Luther King Jr.

18 Thursday

8AM

9

10

11

12

1PM

2

3

4

5

6

19 Friday

8AM

9

10

11

12

1PM

2

3

4

5

6

20 Saturday

21 Sunday

Martin Luther King Jr., "Where Do We Go From Here?" Annual Report Delivered at the 11th Convention of the Southern Christian Leadership Conference, August 16, 1967, Atlanta, Georgia.

AUGUST

S	M	T	W	T	F	S
	1	2	3	4	5	6
7	8	9	10	11	12	13
14	15	16	17	18	19	20
21	22	23	24	25	26	27
28	29	30	31			

SEPTEMBER

S	M	T	W	T	F	S
				1	2	3
4	5	6	7	8	9	10
11	12	13	14	15	16	17
18	19	20	21	22	23	24
25	26	27	28	29	30	

22 Monday

MISSISSIPPI DEMOCRATIC FREEDOM PARTY PROVIDES TESTIMONY ON BLACK VOTING CONCERNS AT DEMOCRATIC NATIONAL CONVENTION, 1964

8AM

9

10

11

12

1PM

2

3

4

5

6

23 Tuesday

8AM

9

10

11

12

1PM

2

3

4

5

6

24 Wednesday

8AM

9

10

11

12

1PM

2

3

4

5

6

MOURNING OUR BLACK CHILDREN

It was hard to bury Emmett Till, hard to bury Carole Robertson, Addie Mae Collins, Denise McNair and Cynthia Wesley, the four girls killed by a bomb in a Birmingham, Alabama, church. So hard an entire nation began to register the convulsions of Black mourning. The deaths of our children in the civil-rights campaigns changed us. Grief was collective; began to unify us, clarify our thinking, roll back the rock of our fear. Emmett Till's mangled face could belong to anybody's Black son who transgressed racial laws; anyone's little girl could be crushed in the rubble of a bombed church. We read the terrorist message inscribed upon Emmett Till's flesh and were shaken, but refused to comply with the terms it set forth.

Because we knew the killing of children was an effort to murder our future, we mourned our young martyrs but also fought with ferocity and dignity in the courts, churches and streets to protect them. Young people, after all, were the shock troops of the movement for social justice, on the front lines, the hottest, most dangerous spots in Alabama and Mississippi. And though they had the most to gain and the most to lose, they also carried on their shoulders the hopes of older generations and generations unborn.

—John Edgar Wideman

John Edgar Wideman, "The Killing of Black Boys," *Essence*, November 1997, 124.

25 Thursday

8AM

9

10

11

12

1PM

2

3

4

5

6

26 Friday

8AM

9

10

11

12

1PM

2

3

4

5

6

27 Saturday

Emmett Till dies 1955

28 Sunday

MARCH ON WASHINGTON, 1963

A TIME TO MARCH

1963. It was a year full of death and tragedy. Blacks in Birmingham faced dogs and fire hoses as they nonviolently battled police chief Eugene "Bull" O'Connor. NAACP Mississippi field secretary Medgar Evers was gunned down in the driveway of his home in Jackson, Miss., and riots broke out in Cambridge, Md. A century after President Lincoln signed the Emancipation Proclamation, Blacks still lived under a brutal system of segregation, treated as second-class citizens without basic human and civil rights.

There was, however, a brilliant moment of hope during that time.

August 28, 1963 was the day that transformed America. It was the culmination of years of boycotts and demonstrations, of freedom rides and sit-ins, of protest and struggle, of sacrifice and suffering. On that day, thousands from around the nation gathered for peace and equality. People of all races stood together as a united front for a single cause. It was called the March on Washington for Jobs and Freedom, yet it was so much more to so many.

There had never been anything like it before, nor anything like it since. It was an extraordinary day that left an even more extraordinary legacy.

—Juan Williams

Juan Williams, "A Time to March," *Crisis (The New)* 110, no. 4 (2003), 23.

AUGUST

S	M	T	W	T	F	S
	1	2	3	4	5	6
7	8	9	10	11	12	13
14	15	16	17	18	19	20
21	22	23	24	25	26	27
28	29	30	31			

SEPTEMBER

S	M	T	W	T	F	S
				1	2	3
4	5	6	7	8	9	10
11	12	13	14	15	16	17
18	19	20	21	22	23	24
25	26	27	28	29	30	

29 Monday

8AM

9

10

11

12

1PM

2

3

4

5

6

30 Tuesday

Roy Wilkins born 1901

8AM

9

10

11

12

1PM

2

3

4

5

6

31 Wednesday

Eldridge Cleaver born 1935

8AM

9

10

11

12

1PM

2

3

4

5

6

THE DESEGREGATION OF LITTLE ROCK

The citizens of Little Rock gathered on September 3 [1957] to gaze upon the incredible spectacle of an empty school building surrounded by 250 National Guard troops. At about eight fifteen in the morning, Central students started passing through the line of national guardsmen—all but the nine Negro students. I had been in touch with their parents throughout the day. They were confused, and they were frightened. As the parents voiced their fears, they kept repeating Governor Faubus' words that "blood would run in the streets of Little Rock" should their teenage children try to attend Central—the school to which they had been assigned by the school board.

—Daisy Bates, president of the Arkansas NAACP and editor-in-chief of the black newspaper the *Arkansas State Press*

1 Thursday

2 Friday

3 Saturday
Charles Hamilton Houston born 1895

1 Thursday

8AM

9

10

11

12

1PM

2

3

4

5

6

2 Friday

8AM

9

10

11

12

1PM

2

3

4

5

6

4 Sunday

Daisy Bates, "The Long Shadow of Little Rock," in *The Eyes on the Prize Civil Rights Reader: Documents, Speeches, and Firsthand Accounts from the Black Freedom Struggle*, edited by Clayborne Carson et al. (New York: Penguin Books, 1991), 97.

AUGUST

S	M	T	W	T	F	S
	1	2	3	4	5	6
7	8	9	10	11	12	13
14	15	16	17	18	19	20
21	22	23	24	25	26	27
28	29	30	31			

SEPTEMBER

S	M	T	W	T	F	S
				1	2	3
4	5	6	7	8	9	10
11	12	13	14	15	16	17
18	19	20	21	22	23	24
25	26	27	28	29	30	

5 Monday
LABOR DAY

8AM

9

10

11

12

1PM

2

3

4

5

6

6 Tuesday

8AM

9

10

11

12

1PM

2

3

4

5

6

7 Wednesday

8AM

9

10

11

12

1PM

2

3

4

5

6

fROM THE COTTON PLANTATIONS TO THE LINCOLN MEMORIAL

IT BEGAN ROUGHLY THREE YEARS BEFORE KING'S speech when blacks walked off cotton plantations in Tennessee and established a tent city of the dispossessed. With the introduction of manmade fibers, cotton faced severe competition. The planters turned the screws of oppression on the black serfs who had kept that industry going since slavery. There was little or no political representation to strengthen their revolt. Blacks had the vote only theoretically. For instance, in some cases, they were asked to recite the entire U.S. Constitution before they could register.

Black revolt spread from Tennessee throughout the south and was joined by black college students across America, and by white students, too. These young people challenged racial discrimination in public places. Soon all America was consumed by the conflict. The demand for a march on Washington grew. To this day, nobody can trace the origins of the idea.

—Darcus Howe

SEPTEMBER 2005

8 Thursday

8AM

9

10

11

12

1PM

2

3

4

5

6

9 Friday

8AM

9

10

11

12

1PM

2

3

4

5

6

10 Saturday

11 Sunday

Darcus Howe, "The U.S. Black Revolt Began on the Cotton Plantations, Not at the Lincoln Memorial," *New Statesman* 132, no. 4654 (2003), 11.

12 Monday

8AM

9

10

11

12

1PM

2

3

4

5

6

13 Tuesday

8AM

9

10

11

12

1PM

2

3

4

5

6

14 Wednesday

8AM

9

10

11

12

1PM

2

3

4

5

6

THE BLISSFUL LIVES OF
FOUR LITTLE GIRLS

Four young black girls arrived at Sunday school, dressed in their usher whites, giggles on their lips, and hair slightly disheveled from gleeful play—ready to learn about Jesus and sing God's praises at their mamas' knees. It was Youth Day at the 16th Street Baptist Church, and even in the midst of the racial turmoil that had seized Birmingham, Ala., they were four little girls living the blissful lives of, well, four little girls.

Hate robbed them of their childhood pleasures. A bomb, planted by a Ku Klux Klansman fiercely opposed to integration, ripped through the basement of their church, sending brick and mortar and furniture hurtling. So strong was the blast that it blew out the face of Jesus in the stained-glass window and stopped the clock.

By the time the chaos had settled into an eerie calm, Carole Denise McNair, 11, and Addie Mae Collins, Cynthia Wesley and Carole Rosamond Robertson, all 14, were dead—buried beneath piles of debris. September 15, 1963, would forever be their day—the day that they became martyrs for the civil rights struggle.

Their deaths changed Alabama—and America, for

15 Thursday

BOMBING AT 16TH STREET BAPTIST CHURCH,
BIRMINGHAM, 1963

8AM

9

10

11

12

1PM

2

3

4

5

6

16 Friday

8AM

9

10

11

12

1PM

2

3

4

5

6

17 Saturday

18 Sunday

that matter. In 1963 Jim Crow ruled the South; Medgar Evers was assassinated; thousands marched on Washington, D.C.; and racists set so many bombs in Birmingham that the predominantly black section of town was called Dynamite Hill. But these four girls were the proof that the civil rights movement needed to show America that racism was destroying the fabric of the United States. Less than a year after they died, Congress pushed through the long-fought-for Civil Rights Act of 1964.

—Denene Millner

SEPTEMBER

S	M	T	W	T	F	S
				1	2	3
4	5	6	7	8	9	10
11	12	13	14	15	16	17
18	19	20	21	22	23	24
25	26	27	28	29	30	

OCTOBER

S	M	T	W	T	F	S
						1
2	3	4	5	6	7	8
9	10	11	12	13	14	15
16	17	18	19	20	21	22
23/30	24/31	25	26	27	28	29

Denene Millner, "Remembering Four Little Girls," *American Visions*, February 1998, 36.

19 Monday

8AM

9

10

11

12

1PM

2

3

4

5

6

20 Tuesday

8AM

9

10

11

12

1PM

2

3

4

5

6

21 Wednesday

8AM

9

10

11

12

1PM

2

3

4

5

6

"A TIME WHEN PEOPLE OF ALL RACES AND ALL WALKS OF LIFE CAME TOGETHER . . ."

Sitting apart on a bus or not being served through the front window of a take-out restaurant was humiliating, but nothing was more painful than being refused a decent education. No matter how much they argued or how long they complained, black families had to send their children to all-black schools no matter how far away. Many buildings were dilapidated, even dangerous. Textbooks were few, worn, and out-of-date; there were no supplies, no afterschool programs, school lunches, sports equipment. Underpaid teachers were overburdened trying to make do.

The demand to integrate public schools grew into a nationwide civil rights movement to eliminate all racist law: to have the right to vote, the right to choose the neighborhood you wanted to live in, to sit in any vacant seat in a public place. Marches, protests, countermarches, and counterprotests erupted almost everywhere. It was an extraordinary time when people of all races and all walks of life came together. When children had to be braver than their parents; when pastors, priests, and rabbis left their altars to walk the streets with strangers; when soldiers with guns were assigned to keep the peace

SEPTEMBER 2005

22 Thursday
AUTUMNAL EQUINOX

8AM

9

10

11

12

1PM

2

3

4

5

6

23 Friday
Mary Church Terrell born 1863

8AM

9

10

11

12

1PM

2

3

4

5

6

24 Saturday
E. Franklin Frazier born 1894

25 Sunday

or to protect a young girl. Days full of loud, angry, determined crowds; and days deep in loneliness. Peaceful marches were met with applause in some places, violence in others. People were hurt and people died. Students and civil rights workers were hosed, beaten, jailed. Strong leaders were shot and killed. And one day a bomb was thrown into a church, killing four little girls attending Sunday school.

—Toni Morrison

SEPTEMBER

S	M	T	W	T	F	S
				1	2	3
4	5	6	7	8	9	10
11	12	13	14	15	16	17
18	19	20	21	22	23	24
25	26	27	28	29	30	

OCTOBER

S	M	T	W	T	F	S
						1
2	3	4	5	6	7	8
9	10	11	12	13	14	15
16	17	18	19	20	21	22
23/30	24/31	25	26	27	28	29

Toni Morrison, "The Journey to School Integration," *Virginia Quarterly Review* 80, no. 1 (2004), 3-4.

26 Monday

27 Tuesday

28 Wednesday
David Walker born 1785

26 Monday	27 Tuesday	28 Wednesday
8AM	8AM	8AM
9	9	9
10	10	10
11	11	11
12	12	12
1PM	1PM	1PM
2	2	2
3	3	3
4	4	4
5	5	5
6	6	6

THE UNEASY TASK OF
DESEGREGATION

DESEGREGATION IS NOT AND WAS NEVER EXPECTED to be an easy task. Racial attitudes ingrained in our Nation's childhood and adolescence are not quickly thrown aside in its middle years. But just as the inconvenience of some cannot be allowed to stand in the way of the rights of others, so public opposition, no matter how strident, cannot be permitted to divert this Court from the enforcement of the constitutional principles at issue in this case. Today's holding, I fear, is more a reflection of a perceived public mood that we have gone far enough in enforcing the Constitution's guarantee of equal justice than it is the product of neutral principles of law. In the short run, it may seem to be the easier course to allow our great metropolitan areas to be divided up each into two cities—one white, the other black—but it is a course, I predict, our people will ultimately regret. I dissent.

—Justice Thurgood Marshall

29 Thursday

8AM

9

10

11

12

1PM

2

3

4

5

6

30 Friday

8AM

9

10

11

12

1PM

2

3

4

5

6

1 Saturday

2 Sunday

THURGOOD MARSHALL SWORN IN AS
SUPREME COURT JUSTICE, 1967
Nat Turner born 1800

Thurgood Marshall, *Miliken vs. Bradley,* 418 U.S. 717 (1974) at 814-815.

SEPTEMBER

S	M	T	W	T	F	S
				1	2	3
4	5	6	7	8	9	10
11	12	13	14	15	16	17
18	19	20	21	22	23	24
25	26	27	28	29	30	

OCTOBER

S	M	T	W	T	F	S
						1
2	3	4	5	6	7	8
9	10	11	12	13	14	15
16	17	18	19	20	21	22
23/30	24/31	25	26	27	28	29

3 Monday

ROSH HASHANAH BEGINS AT SUNDOWN
T. Thomas Fortune born 1856

8AM

9

10

11

12

1PM

2

3

4

5

6

4 Tuesday

8AM

9

10

11

12

1PM

2

3

4

5

6

5 Wednesday

Autherine Lucy Foster born 1929

8AM

9

10

11

12

1PM

2

3

4

5

6

WHERE THE RAGE GOES

I remember treating Negro workers after they had been beaten viciously by white toughs or policemen while conducting civil rights demonstrations. I would frequently comment, "You must feel pretty angry getting beaten up like that by those bigots." Often I received a reply such as: "No, I don't hate those white men, I love them because they must really be suffering with all that hatred in their souls. Dr. King says the only way we can win our freedom is through love. Anger and hatred has never solved anything."

I used to sit there and wonder, "Now, what do they really do with their rage?"

While they were talking about being nonviolent and "loving" the sheriff that just hit them over the head, they rampaged around the project houses beating up each other. I frequently had to calm Negro civil rights workers with large doses of tranquilizers for what I can describe clinically only as acute attacks of rage.

This rage was at a fever pitch for many months, before it became crystallized in the "Black Power" slogan. The workers who shouted it loudest were those with the oldest battle scars from the terror, demoralization, and castration which they experienced

OCTOBER 2005

6 Thursday
Fannie Lou Hamer born 1917

8AM

9

10

11

12

1PM

2

3

4

5

6

7 Friday

8AM

9

10

11

12

1PM

2

3

4

5

6

8 Saturday
Jesse Jackson born 1941

9 Sunday

through continual direct confrontation with Southern white racists. Furthermore, some of the most bellicose chanters of the slogan had been, just a few years before, examples of nonviolent, loving passive resistance in their struggle against white supremacy. The workers appeared to be seeking a sense of inner psychological emancipation from racists through self-assertion and release of aggressive angry feelings.

—Alvin F. Poussaint

Alvin F. Poussaint, "A Negro Psychiatrist Explains the Negro Psyche," *The New York Times Magazine*, August 20, 1967, 55.

OCTOBER

S	M	T	W	T	F	S
						1
2	3	4	5	6	7	8
9	10	11	12	13	14	15
16	17	18	19	20	21	22
23/30	24/31	25	26	27	28	29

NOVEMBER

S	M	T	W	T	F	S
		1	2	3	4	5
6	7	8	9	10	11	12
13	14	15	16	17	18	19
20	21	22	23	24	25	26
27	28	29	30			

10 Monday
COLUMBUS DAY OBSERVED
THANKSGIVING (CANADA)

8AM

9

10

11

12

1PM

2

3

4

5

6

11 Tuesday

8AM

9

10

11

12

1PM

2

3

4

5

6

12 Wednesday
YOM KIPPUR BEGINS AT SUNDOWN
ANGELA Y. DAVIS ARRESTED ON
KIDNAPPING, MURDER, AND CONSPIRACY
CHARGES, 1970

8AM

9

10

11

12

1PM

2

3

4

5

6

"WE SOUGHT SOLIDARITY. WE CALLED FOR BLACK POWER . . ."

Those of us who were drawn to the early Black Panther Party were just one more insurgent band of young men and women who refused to tolerate the systematic violence and abuse being meted out to poor blacks, to middle class blacks, and any old ordinary blacks. When we looked at our situation, when we saw violence, bad housing, unemployment, rotten education, unfair treatment in the courts, as well as the direct attacks from the police, our response was to defend ourselves. We became part of that assault against the capitalist powers.

In a world of racist polarization, we sought solidarity. We called for black power for black people, red power for red people, brown power for brown people, yellow power for yellow people, and, as Eldridge Cleaver used to say, white power for white people, because all they'd known is "Pig power." We organized the Rainbow Coalition, pulled together our allies including not only the Puerto Rican Young Lords, the youth gang called the Black P Stone Rangers, the Chicano Brown Berets, the Asian I Wor Keun (Red Guards) but also the predominantly white Peace and Freedom Party, and the Appalachian Young Patriots Party. We posed not only a theoretical but a practical challenge to the way our world was organized. And we were men and women working together.

—Kathleen Neal Cleaver

OCTOBER 2005

13 Thursday

8AM

9

10

11

12

1PM

2

3

4

5

6

14 Friday

8AM

9

10

11

12

1PM

2

3

4

5

6

15 Saturday

HUEY P. NEWTON AND BOBBY SEALE DRAFT
THE FIRST VERSION OF THE TEN-POINT
PROGRAM, WHICH ESTABLISHES THE BLACK
PANTHER PARTY FOR SELF DEFENSE, 1966

16 Sunday

OCTOBER

S	M	T	W	T	F	S
						1
2	3	4	5	6	7	8
9	10	11	12	13	14	15
16	17	18	19	20	21	22
23/30	24/31	25	26	27	28	29

NOVEMBER

S	M	T	W	T	F	S
		1	2	3	4	5
6	7	8	9	10	11	12
13	14	15	16	17	18	19
20	21	22	23	24	25	26
27	28	29	30			

Kathleen Neal Cleaver, "Women, Power, and Revolution," *New Political Science* 21, no. 2 (1999), 233.

17 Monday

8AM

9

10

11

12

1PM

2

3

4

5

6

18 Tuesday

8AM

9

10

11

12

1PM

2

3

4

5

6

19 Wednesday

8AM

9

10

11

12

1PM

2

3

4

5

6

POWER TO THE PEOPLE

We must educate the people more broadly about the people's revolutionary movement, and about the people's struggle to end war, racism and repression. Of course, we revolutionary, peace-loving people who want to end war, racism and repression know the general outlines of what we must attempt to do to help make a peace-loving society and world. We must make more widely known what we believe in for the people, all the people, beyond our beautiful rhetoric of "All Power to the People."

—Bobby Seale and Ericka Huggins

20 Thursday

8AM

9

10

11

12

1PM

2

3

4

5

6

21 Friday

8AM

9

10

11

12

1PM

2

3

4

5

6

22 Saturday

Bobby Seale born 1936

23 Sunday

JACKIE ROBINSON BECOMES THE FIRST BLACK BASEBALL PLAYER TO SIGN A FORMAL MAJOR LEAGUE CONTRACT, 1945

OCTOBER

S	M	T	W	T	F	S
						1
2	3	4	5	6	7	8
9	10	11	12	13	14	15
16	17	18	19	20	21	22
23/30	24/31	25	26	27	28	29

NOVEMBER

S	M	T	W	T	F	S
		1	2	3	4	5
6	7	8	9	10	11	12
13	14	15	16	17	18	19
20	21	22	23	24	25	26
27	28	29	30			

Bobby Seale and Ericka Huggins, "A Message from Prison," in Angela Y. Davis, *If They Come in the Morning: Voices of Resistance* (New York: Signet Classics, 1971), 121-122.

24 Monday
Kweisi Mfume born 1948
Jackie Robinson dies 1972

8AM

9

10

11

12

1PM

2

3

4

5

6

25 Tuesday

8AM

9

10

11

12

1PM

2

3

4

5

6

26 Wednesday
Robert Reed Church Jr. born 1885

8AM

9

10

11

12

1PM

2

3

4

5

6

"17 MILLION NEGROES CANNOT DO AS YOU SUGGEST"

My Dear Mr. President:

I was sitting in the audience at the Summit Meeting of Negro Leaders yesterday when you said we must have patience. On hearing you say this, I felt like standing up and saying, "Oh no! Not again."

I respectfully remind you sir, that we have been the most patient of all people. When you say we must have self-respect, I wondered how we could have self-respect and remain patient considering the treatment accorded us through the years.

17 million Negroes cannot do as you suggest and wait for the hearts of men to change. We want to enjoy now the rights that we feel we are entitled to as Americans. This we cannot do unless we pursue aggressively goals which all other Americans achieved over 150 years ago.

As the chief executive of our nation, I respectfully suggest that you unwittingly crush the spirit of freedom in Negroes by constantly urging forbearance and give hope to those pro-segregation leaders like Governor [Orval] Faubus who would take from us

27 Thursday

8AM

9

10

11

12

1PM

2

3

4

5

6

28 Friday

8AM

9

10

11

12

1PM

2

3

4

5

6

29 Saturday

30 Sunday

DAYLIGHT SAVING TIME ENDS

those freedoms we now enjoy. Your own experience with Governor Faubus is proof enough that forbearance and not eventual integration is the goal the pro-segregation leaders seek.

In my view, an unequivocal statement backed up by action such as you demonstrated you could take last fall in dealing with Governor Faubus (in Little Rock, Arkansas) if it became necessary, would let it be known that America is determined to provide—in the near future—for Negroes—the freedoms we are entitled to under the Constitution.

—Jackie Robinson

Jackie Robinson to President Dwight D. Eisenhower, dated May 13, 1958. Letter to the President. Dwight D. Eisenhower Library, White House Central Files, Box 731 File: OF-142-A-3.

OCTOBER

S	M	T	W	T	F	S
						1
2	3	4	5	6	7	8
9	10	11	12	13	14	15
16	17	18	19	20	21	22
23/30	24/31	25	26	27	28	29

NOVEMBER

S	M	T	W	T	F	S
		1	2	3	4	5
6	7	8	9	10	11	12
13	14	15	16	17	18	19
20	21	22	23	24	25	26
27	28	29	30			

31 Monday
HALLOWEEN

8AM

9

10

11

12

1PM

2

3

4

5

6

1 Tuesday

8AM

9

10

11

12

1PM

2

3

4

5

6

2 Wednesday

8AM

9

10

11

12

1PM

2

3

4

5

6

"A PROPOSAL THAT . . . MUST BECOME PART OF THE BASIC LAW OF THE LAND"

AS A BLACK PERSON, I AM NO STRANGER TO RACE PREJUDICE. But the truth is that in the political world I have been far oftener discriminated against because I am a woman than because I am black.

Prejudice against blacks is becoming unacceptable although it will take years to eliminate it. But it is doomed because, slowly, white America is beginning to admit that it exists. Prejudice against women is still acceptable. There is very little understanding yet of the immorality involved in double pay scales and the classification of most of the better jobs as "for men only."

More than half of the population of the United States is female. But women occupy only two percent of the managerial positions. They have not even reached the level of tokenism yet. No women sit on the AFL-CIO council or Supreme Court. There have been only two women who have held Cabinet rank, and at present there are none. Only two women now hold ambassadorial rank in the diplomatic corps. In Congress, we are down to one senator and ten representatives.

Considering that there are about three-and-a-half million more women in the United States than men, this situation is outrageous! It is true that part of the problem has been that women have not been aggressive in demanding their rights. This was also true of the black population for many years. They submitted to oppression

OCTOBER-NOVEMBER 2005

3 Thursday

8AM

9

10

11

12

1PM

2

3

4

5

6

4 Friday

8AM

9

10

11

12

1PM

2

3

4

5

6

5 Saturday

SHIRLEY CHISHOLM ELECTED AMERICA'S
FIRST BLACK WOMAN TO CONGRESS, 1968

6 Sunday

and even cooperated with it. Women have done the same thing. But now there is an awareness of this situation particularly among the younger segment of the population.

As in the field of equal rights for blacks, Spanish-Americans, the Indians, and other groups, laws will not change such deep-seated problems overnight. But they can be used to provide protection for those who are most abused, and to begin the process of evolutionary change by compelling the insensitive majority to reexamine its unconscious attitudes.

It is for this reason that I wish to introduce today a proposal that has been before every Congress for the last 40 years and that sooner or later must become part of the basic law of the land—the Equal Rights Amendment.

—Representative Shirley Chisholm (D-NY)
urges her House colleagues to pass
the Equal Rights Amendment,
Washington, D.C., May 21, 1969

OCTOBER

S	M	T	W	T	F	S
						1
2	3	4	5	6	7	8
9	10	11	12	13	14	15
16	17	18	19	20	21	22
23/30	24/31	25	26	27	28	29

NOVEMBER

S	M	T	W	T	F	S
		1	2	3	4	5
6	7	8	9	10	11	12
13	14	15	16	17	18	19
20	21	22	23	24	25	26
27	28	29	30			

7 Monday

INTERSTATE COMMERCE COMMISSION RULES THAT SEGREGATED SEATING ON INTERSTATE BUSES AND TRAINS IS A VIOLATION OF THE INTERSTATE COMMERCE ACT, 1956

8AM

9

10

11

12

1PM

2

3

4

5

6

8 Tuesday

ELECTION DAY

8AM

9

10

11

12

1PM

2

3

4

5

6

9 Wednesday

8AM

9

10

11

12

1PM

2

3

4

5

6

"NOT AMERICAN NEGRO, ARE YOU?"

I have just come out of the South, having been during this lecture season from the Carolinas to Texas. On some trains heading southward from Washington through Virginia, I have been served without difficulty at any table in the diner, with white passengers eating with me. Further South, I have encountered the curtain, behind which I had to sit in order to eat, often being served with the colored Pullman porters and brakemen. On other trains there has been no curtain and no intention for Negroes to eat.

Coming out of Chattanooga on such a train, I went into the diner on the first call for dinner because sometimes these days if you wait for the second call everything will be gone. As I entered the diner, I said to the white steward, "One, please." He looked at me in amazement and walked off toward the other end of the car. The diner was filling rapidly, but there were still a couple of empty tables in the center of the car, so I went ahead and sat down.

Three whites soon joined me, then all the seats in

10 Thursday

8AM

9

10

11

12

1PM

2

3

4

5

6

11 Friday
VETERANS DAY
REMEMBRANCE DAY (CANADA)
Shirley Graham Du Bois born 1896

8AM

9

10

11

12

1PM

2

3

4

5

6

12 Saturday

13 Sunday

the dining car were taken. The steward came and gave the three whites menus, but ignored me. Every time he passed, though, he would look at me and frown. Finally he leaned over and whispered in my ear.

"Say, fellow, are you Puerto Rican?"

"No," I said, "I'm American."

"Not American Negro, are you?" he demanded.

"I'm just hungry," I said loudly.

He gave me a menu! The colored waiters grinned. They served me with great courtesy, a quality which I have always found our dining car waiters to possess.

—Langston Hughes

Langston Hughes, "Adventures in Dining," *The Chicago Defender*, June 2, 1945.

NOVEMBER

S	M	T	W	T	F	S
		1	2	3	4	5
6	7	8	9	10	11	12
13	14	15	16	17	18	19
20	21	22	23	24	25	26
27	28	29	30			

DECEMBER

S	M	T	W	T	F	S
				1	2	3
4	5	6	7	8	9	10
11	12	13	14	15	16	17
18	19	20	21	22	23	24
25	26	27	28	29	30	31

14 Monday

8AM

9

10

11

12

1PM

2

3

4

5

6

15 Tuesday

8AM

9

10

11

12

1PM

2

3

4

5

6

16 Wednesday

8AM

9

10

11

12

1PM

2

3

4

5

6

"THESE IMAGES...CHANGED THE PERCEPTION THAT THE UNITED STATES HAD OF ITSELF"

FOR THE CIVIL RIGHTS MOVEMENT THE REVOLUTION WAS televised. Beginning with the Little Rock Crisis in 1957, almost all of the key moments of the Civil Rights Movement in the late fifties and early sixties were caught by television cameras. By broadcasting what happened, these images, some orchestrated, such as the March on Washington, and some, like "Bloody Sunday" in Selma, totally spontaneous, changed the perception that the United States had of itself.

Even in the South the difference was felt. In 1955 only twenty percent of those polled were in favor of school desegregation, but in 1964 sixty-two percent of Southerners favored the civil rights bill as long as it was implemented gradually. This was a staggering change of heart, especially to come about in just over a decade. In Albany [Georgia], the Civil Rights Movement suffered defeat thanks to the tactics of Sheriff Laurie Prichett. However, it was this failure that led to the later more successful campaigns in Birmingham and Selma. The Albany campaign showed King what was necessary to bring national attention to the segregated South. He needed headlines that demonstrated the cruelty and injustice of segregation. While Albany in and of itself was not a victory for the movement, it did provide the education that led to the success in Birmingham.

17 Thursday
ALBANY MOVEMENT FORMED, 1961

18 Friday
Howard Thurman born 1900

19 Saturday

8AM

9

10

11

12

1PM

2

3

4

5

6

8AM

9

10

11

12

1PM

2

3

4

5

6

20 Sunday

The Birmingham campaign was the most important campaign of the modern Civil Rights Movement. While the concessions made by the city were small, it was this campaign that led to the passage of the Civil Rights Act of 1964. Bull Connor lost all control over the city as well as any credibility he had when the national media caught the images and events of the "D-Day" demonstrations. With the nation finally understanding what the South was perpetuating with segregation, the system of depriving people of their rights very quickly eroded.

—Kyle T. Scanlan

NOVEMBER

S	M	T	W	T	F	S
		1	2	3	4	5
6	7	8	9	10	11	12
13	14	15	16	17	18	19
20	21	22	23	24	25	26
27	28	29	30			

DECEMBER

S	M	T	W	T	F	S
				1	2	3
4	5	6	7	8	9	10
11	12	13	14	15	16	17
18	19	20	21	22	23	24
25	26	27	28	29	30	31

Kyle T. Scanlan, "Fight the Power: Protest, Showdown and Civil Rights Activity in Three Southern Cities, 1960-1965" (master's thesis, East Tennessee State University, 2001), 92-94.

21 Monday

8AM

9

10

11

12

1PM

2

3

4

5

6

22 Tuesday

8AM

9

10

11

12

1PM

2

3

4

5

6

23 Wednesday

8AM

9

10

11

12

1PM

2

3

4

5

6

"THE INEVITABLE NEW ORDER OF JUSTICE IN THE SOUTH AND ALL THE UNITED STATES"

Albany was an inspired, honest, and united nonviolent Negro uprising without previous tactical experience. I think the Albany Movement blazed a trail in pragmatic experience and endured an ordeal which was, and is, a big beginning in the Deep South. I also believe that this Movement lit a fire which cannot be extinguished, though it has stages of temporary defeat and frustration. But the beat and high aspiration are unquenched. . . .

The Negro community will never again return willingly and despairingly to segregation. And their sacrificial summer of 1962 will influence the fight on segregation wherever it exists.

It is, I believe, no "failure" when a united Negro community drives and sacrifices for nearly two years to assert and demand its rights. People who make such assertions and endure such persecution are by no means defeated or broken. They will never succumb and their sacrifice is an offering to the inevitable new order of justice in the South and all the United States.

The "defeat" of Albany is, then, a protest and

24 Thursday
THANKSGIVING

8AM

9

10

11

12

1PM

2

3

4

5

6

25 Friday

8AM

9

10

11

12

1PM

2

3

4

5

6

26 Saturday

27 Sunday
MARTIN LUTHER KING JR. ANNOUNCES THE INCEPTION OF THE POOR PEOPLE'S CAMPAIGN, FOCUSING ON JOBS AND FREEDOM FOR THE POOR OF ALL RACES, 1967

---

penalty in necessary demonstration and suffering which has obviously changed Albany and inspired other Negro communities, as it has warned and cautioned white authorities elsewhere in the South.

In the words of Marion King, an Albany mother who has given and lost a great deal to the Movement, the community has now "this vision and this faith in freedom that will not die and cannot be stopped."

—Rev. Wyatt Tee Walker

NOVEMBER

S	M	T	W	T	F	S
		1	2	3	4	5
6	7	8	9	10	11	12
13	14	15	16	17	18	19
20	21	22	23	24	25	26
27	28	29	30			

DECEMBER

S	M	T	W	T	F	S
				1	2	3
4	5	6	7	8	9	10
11	12	13	14	15	16	17
18	19	20	21	22	23	24
25	26	27	28	29	30	31

Wyatt Tee Walker, "Albany, Future or First Step?" in *Gonna Sit at the Welcome Table*, edited by Julian Bond and Andrew Lewis (Mason, OH: Thompson Learning Group Custom Publishing, 2002), 522-525.

28 Monday

8AM

9

10

11

12

1PM

2

3

4

5

6

29 Tuesday
Adam Clayton Powell Jr. born 1908

8AM

9

10

11

12

1PM

2

3

4

5

6

30 Wednesday
Shirley Chisholm born 1924

8AM

9

10

11

12

1PM

2

3

4

5

6

WE STILL LOVE TO HEAR HER STORY

WE KNOW THE STORY. ONE EVENING, A WOMAN LEFT work and boarded a bus for home. She was tired; her feet ached. But this was Montgomery, Alabama, in 1955, and as the bus became crowded, the woman, a black woman, was ordered to give up her seat to a white passenger. When she remained seated, that simple decision eventually led to the disintegration of institutionalized segregation in the South, ushering in a new era of the civil rights movement.

This, anyway, was the story I had heard from the time I was curious enough to eavesdrop on adult conversations. I was three years old when a white bus driver warned Rosa Parks, "Well, I'm going to have you arrested" and she replied, "You may go on and do so." As a child, I didn't understand how doing nothing had caused so much activity, but I recognized the template: David slaying the giant Goliath, or the boy who saved his village by sticking his finger in the dike. And perhaps it is precisely the lure of fairy-tale retribution that colors the lens we look back through. Parks was 42 years old when she refused to give up her seat. She has insisted that her feet were not aching; she was, by her own testimony, no more tired than usual. And she did not plan her fateful act: "I did not get on the bus

1 Thursday

ROSA PARKS ARRESTED FOR REFUSING TO
MOVE TO THE BACK OF THE BUS, 1955

8AM

9

10

11

12

1PM

2

3

4

5

6

2 Friday

8AM

9

10

11

12

1PM

2

3

4

5

6

3 Saturday

4 Sunday

to get arrested" she has said. "I got on the bus to go home."

Montgomery's segregation laws were complex: blacks were required to pay their fare to the driver, then get off and reboard through the back door. Sometimes the bus would drive off before the paid-up customers made it to the back entrance. If the white section was full and another white customer entered, blacks were required to give up their seats and move farther to the back; a black person was not even allowed to sit across the aisle from whites. These humiliations were compounded by the fact that two-thirds of the bus riders in Montgomery were black.

—Rita Dove

Rita Dove, "The Torchbearer Rosa Parks," *Literary Cavalcade* 52, no. 5 (2000), 14.

NOVEMBER

S	M	T	W	T	F	S
		1	2	3	4	5
6	7	8	9	10	11	12
13	14	15	16	17	18	19
20	21	22	23	24	25	26
27	28	29	30			

DECEMBER

S	M	T	W	T	F	S
				1	2	3
4	5	6	7	8	9	10
11	12	13	14	15	16	17
18	19	20	21	22	23	24
25	26	27	28	29	30	31

5 Monday

NATIONAL COUNCIL OF NEGRO WOMEN
FOUNDED, 1935
MONTGOMERY BUS BOYCOTT BEGINS, 1955

8AM

9

10

11

12

1PM

2

3

4

5

6

6 Tuesday

8AM

9

10

11

12

1PM

2

3

4

5

6

7 Wednesday

8AM

9

10

11

12

1PM

2

3

4

5

6

"STRANGE FRUIT"

Billie Holiday's recording of "Strange Fruit" achieved something far greater than the permanent preservation of her most important song, the aesthetic centerpiece of her career. Eventually, millions heard her sing this haunting anti-lynching appeal—more people than she herself would ever have imagined. She could not have predicted that "Strange Fruit" would impel people to discover within themselves a previously unawakened calling to political activism, but it did, and it does. She could not have foreseen the catalytic role her song would play in rejuvenating the tradition of protest and resistance in African-American and American traditions of popular music and culture. Nevertheless, Billie Holiday's recording of "Strange Fruit" persists as one of the most influential and profound examples—and continuing sites—of the intersection of music and social consciousness.

"Strange Fruit" was a frontal challenge not only to lynching and racism but to the policies of a government that implicitly condoned such activities especially through its refusal to pass laws against lynching. The song was thus an undisguised rallying cry against the state.

—Angela Y. Davis

DECEMBER 2005

8 Thursday

8AM

9

10

11

12

1PM

2

3

4

5

6

9 Friday

8AM

9

10

11

12

1PM

2

3

4

5

6

10 Saturday

RALPH BUNCHE AWARDED NOBEL PEACE PRIZE, 1950
MARTIN LUTHER KING JR. AWARDED NOBEL PEACE PRIZE, 1964

11 Sunday

Angela Y. Davis, *Blues Legacies and Black Feminism: Gertrude Ma Rainey, Bessie Smith, and Billie Holiday* (New York: Pantheon Books, 1999), 196-197.

DECEMBER

S	M	T	W	T	F	S
				1	2	3
4	5	6	7	8	9	10
11	12	13	14	15	16	17
18	19	20	21	22	23	24
25	26	27	28	29	30	31

JANUARY

S	M	T	W	T	F	S
1	2	3	4	5	6	7
8	9	10	11	12	13	14
15	16	17	18	19	20	21
22	23	24	25	26	27	28
29	30	31				

12 Monday

8AM

9

10

11

12

1PM

2

3

4

5

6

13 Tuesday

8AM

9

10

11

12

1PM

2

3

4

5

6

14 Wednesday

8AM

9

10

11

12

1PM

2

3

4

5

6

"A NEW TIME HAD COME...ALL OVER THE NONWHITE WORLD"

Why did it happen with such momentum in those years? Because there were black churches, often built in the hard, post-Reconstruction days, where rallies, mobilizing, and planning could now take place. Because black (and a few white) ministers were willing to stand firm on the front lines against the moral evil of segregation and call their people to do the same, regardless of the cost.

It happened because white American leaders knew the cold war-conscious world was watching a nation that dared call itself "the leader of the free world" to see how it would deal with its own citizens who had so long clamored for freedom.

It happened because the post-World War II generation of men and women were the first African-Americans who grew to their maturity in a world where the power, hegemony, and wisdom of the European world were everywhere being publicly questioned, rejected, and attacked. They knew a new time had come, was coming, all over the nonwhite world, and that they were related to it all. At great personal risk and cost, Du Bois, Paul Robeson, Lena Horne, and others kept reminding black people of their relationship to this vaster world of men and women struggling for transformation.

—Vincent Harding

15 Thursday

8AM

9

10

11

12

1PM

2

3

4

5

6

16 Friday

MARTIN LUTHER KING JR., RALPH ABERNATHY,
AND 264 OTHER PROTESTERS ARE
ARRESTED DURING A CAMPAIGN
IN ALBANY, GEORGIA, 1961

8AM

9

10

11

12

1PM

2

3

4

5

6

17 Saturday

18 Sunday

Vincent Harding in *The Eyes on the Prize Civil Rights Reader: Documents, Speeches, and Firsthand Accounts from the Black Freedom Struggle*, edited by Clayborne Carson, Vincent Harding et al. (New York: Penguin Books, 1991), 33.

DECEMBER

S	M	T	W	T	F	S
				1	2	3
4	5	6	7	8	9	10
11	12	13	14	15	16	17
18	19	20	21	22	23	24
25	26	27	28	29	30	31

JANUARY

S	M	T	W	T	F	S
1	2	3	4	5	6	7
8	9	10	11	12	13	14
15	16	17	18	19	20	21
22	23	24	25	26	27	28
29	30	31				

19 Monday
Carter G. Woodson born 1875

20 Tuesday
William Julius Wilson born 1935

21 Wednesday
WINTER SOLSTICE
MONTGOMERY BUS
BOYCOTT ENDS, 1956

8AM	8AM	8AM
9	9	9
10	10	10
11	11	11
12	12	12
1PM	1PM	1PM
2	2	2
3	3	3
4	4	4
5	5	5
6	6	6

"AT KEY JUNCTURES PEOPLE ALWAYS STEPPED UP"

During the years of struggle thousands and thousands of people made impressive sacrifices . . . as one example of the effect [of the yearlong Montgomery bus boycott] on people's lives, one participant walked 11 miles to work every day of the boycott, worked at physical labor, and walked 11 miles home (King 1958). Many people who participated in the civil rights movement lost their lives; many more lost their jobs or were evicted from their homes or were brutally beaten.

Crucial to the success of the movement was the fact that at key junctures people always stepped up, volunteering to run serious risks and to make sacrifices that no one could reasonably have demanded of them. The leaders of the movement led by example, putting themselves in the front line. At certain historic confrontations virtually the entire Black population of some locality supported the movement, and supported it not just through passive verbal support, but also in active participation and sacrifice, despite inconvenience, arrest, and physical danger.

—Aldon Morris and Dan Clawson

22 Thursday

8AM

9

10

11

12

1PM

2

3

4

5

6

23 Friday

8AM

9

10

11

12

1PM

2

3

4

5

6

24 Saturday

25 Sunday

HANUKKAH BEGINS AT SUNDOWN
CHRISTMAS

DECEMBER

S	M	T	W	T	F	S
				1	2	3
4	5	6	7	8	9	10
11	12	13	14	15	16	17
18	19	20	21	22	23	24
25	26	27	28	29	30	31

JANUARY

S	M	T	W	T	F	S
1	2	3	4	5	6	7
8	9	10	11	12	13	14
15	16	17	18	19	20	21
22	23	24	25	26	27	28
29	30	31				

Aldon Morris and Dan Clawson, "Lessons of the Civil Rights Movement for Workers' Rights/Union Organizing," Prepared for Presentation at the AFL-CIO/Michigan State University Worker Rights Conference, Kellogg Center, Michigan State University, East Lansing, MI, Oct. 11-12, 2002, 23-24.

26 Monday
1ST DAY OF KWANZAA

8AM

9

10

11

12

1PM

2

3

4

5

6

27 Tuesday
2ND DAY OF KWANZAA

8AM

9

10

11

12

1PM

2

3

4

5

6

28 Wednesday
3RD DAY OF KWANZAA

8AM

9

10

11

12

1PM

2

3

4

5

6

THE TRANSFORMATIVE POTENTIAL OF NONVIOLENCE

WE AFFIRM THE PHILOSOPHICAL AND RELIGIOUS ideal of nonviolence as the foundation of our purpose, the pre-supposition of our faith, and the manner of our action. Nonviolence as it grows from Judaic-Christian traditions seeks a social order of justice permeated by love. Integration of human endeavor represents the crucial first step towards such a society.

Through nonviolence, courage displaces fear; love transforms hate. Acceptance dissipates prejudice; hope ends despair. Peace eliminates war; faith reconciles doubt. Mutual regard cancels disunity. Justice for all overthrows injustice. The redemptive community supersedes systems of gross social immorality.

Love is the central motif of nonviolence. Love is the force by which God binds man to himself and man to man. Such love goes to the extreme; it remains loving and forgiving even in the midst of hostility. It matches the capacity of evil to inflict suffering with an even more enduring capacity to absorb evil, all the while persisting in love.

29 Thursday
4TH DAY OF KWANZAA

8AM

9

10

11

12

1PM

2

3

4

5

6

30 Friday
5TH DAY OF KWANZAA

8AM

9

10

11

12

1PM

2

3

4

5

6

31 Saturday
NEW YEAR'S EVE
6TH DAY OF KWANZAA

1 Sunday
NEW YEAR'S DAY
7TH DAY OF KWANZAA

By appealing to conscience and standing on the moral nature of human existence, nonviolence nurtures the atmosphere in which reconciliation and justice become actual possibilities.

— Student Nonviolent Coordinating Committee Statement of Purpose, April 15, 1960.

"Student Nonviolent Coordinating Committee Statement of Purpose," in *The Eyes on the Prize Civil Rights Reader: Documents, Speeches, and Firsthand Accounts from the Black Freedom Struggle*, edited by Clayborne Carson et al. (New York: Penguin Books, 1991), 119.

DECEMBER

S	M	T	W	T	F	S
				1	2	3
4	5	6	7	8	9	10
11	12	13	14	15	16	17
18	19	20	21	22	23	24
25	26	27	28	29	30	31

JANUARY

S	M	T	W	T	F	S
1	2	3	4	5	6	7
8	9	10	11	12	13	14
15	16	17	18	19	20	21
22	23	24	25	26	27	28
29	30	31				

2 Monday

8AM

9

10

11

12

1PM

2

3

4

5

6

3 Tuesday

8AM

9

10

11

12

1PM

2

3

4

5

6

4 Wednesday

8AM

9

10

11

12

1PM

2

3

4

5

6

5 Thursday

6 Friday

7 Saturday

| 8AM |
| 9 |
| 10 |
| 11 |
| 12 |
| 1PM |
| 2 |
| 3 |
| 4 |
| 5 |
| 6 |

| 8AM |
| 9 |
| 10 |
| 11 |
| 12 |
| 1PM |
| 2 |
| 3 |
| 4 |
| 5 |
| 6 |

8 Sunday

DECEMBER

S	M	T	W	T	F	S
				1	2	3
4	5	6	7	8	9	10
11	12	13	14	15	16	17
18	19	20	21	22	23	24
25	26	27	28	29	30	31

JANUARY

S	M	T	W	T	F	S
1	2	3	4	5	6	7
8	9	10	11	12	13	14
15	16	17	18	19	20	21
22	23	24	25	26	27	28
29	30	31				

2006 Planner

JANUARY

S	M	T	W	T	F	S
1	2	3	4	5	6	7
8	9	10	11	12	13	14
15	16	17	18	19	20	21
22	23	24	25	26	27	28
29	30	31				

FEBRUARY

S	M	T	W	T	F	S
			1	2	3	4
5	6	7	8	9	10	11
12	13	14	15	16	17	18
19	20	21	22	23	24	25
26	27	28				

MARCH

S	M	T	W	T	F	S
			1	2	3	4
5	6	7	8	9	10	11
12	13	14	15	16	17	18
19	20	21	22	23	24	25
26	27	28	29	30	31	

2006 Planner

APRIL

S	M	T	W	T	F	S
						1
2	3	4	5	6	7	8
9	10	11	12	13	14	15
16	17	18	19	20	21	22
23/30	24	25	26	27	28	29

MAY

S	M	T	W	T	F	S
	1	2	3	4	5	6
7	8	9	10	11	12	13
14	15	16	17	18	19	20
21	22	23	24	25	26	27
28	29	30	31			

JUNE

S	M	T	W	T	F	S
				1	2	3
4	5	6	7	8	9	10
11	12	13	14	15	16	17
18	19	20	21	22	23	24
25	26	27	28	29	30	

2006 Planner

JULY

S	M	T	W	T	F	S
						1
2	3	4	5	6	7	8
9	10	11	12	13	14	15
16	17	18	19	20	21	22
23/30	24/31	25	26	27	28	29

AUGUST

S	M	T	W	T	F	S
		1	2	3	4	5
6	7	8	9	10	11	12
13	14	15	16	17	18	19
20	21	22	23	24	25	26
27	28	29	30	31		

SEPTEMBER

S	M	T	W	T	F	S
					1	2
3	4	5	6	7	8	9
10	11	12	13	14	15	16
17	18	19	20	21	22	23
24	25	26	27	28	29	30

2006 Planner

OCTOBER

S	M	T	W	T	F	S
1	2	3	4	5	6	7
8	9	10	11	12	13	14
15	16	17	18	19	20	21
22	23	24	25	26	27	28
29	30	31				

NOVEMBER

S	M	T	W	T	F	S
			1	2	3	4
5	6	7	8	9	10	11
12	13	14	15	16	17	18
19	20	21	22	23	24	25
26	27	28	29	30		

DECEMBER

S	M	T	W	T	F	S
					1	2
3	4	5	6	7	8	9
10	11	12	13	14	15	16
17	18	19	20	21	22	23
24/31	25	26	27	28	29	30

Toll-Free Numbers and Websites

CREDIT CARDS (LOST OR STOLEN)

AMERICAN EXPRESS *www.americanexpress.com*

    USA 800-528-4800

    Canada 800-263-9222

MASTERCARD *www.mastercard.com*

    USA & Canada 800-307-7309

VISA *www.visa.com*

    USA & Canada 800-847-2911

U.S. AIRLINES

American *www.americanairlines.com* 800-433-7300

America West *www.americawest.com* 800-235-9292

Continental *www.continental.com* 800-525-0280

Delta *www.delta.com* 800-221-1212

Northwest *www.nwa.com* 800-225-2525

United *www.united.com* 800-241-6522

USAirways *www.usairways.com* 800-428-4322

INTERNATIONAL AIRLINES

Aero Mexico *www.aeromexico.com* 800-237-6639

Air Canada *www.aircanada.ca* 888-247-2262

Air Jamaica *www.airjamaica.com* 800-523-5585

British Airways *www.british-airways.com* 800-247-9297

Finnair *www.finnair.com* 800-950-5000

Iberia Airlines *www.iberia.com* 800-772-4642

Icelandair *www.icelandair.is* 800-223-5500

Japan Air Lines *www.japanair.com* 800-525-3663

KLM *www.klm.nl* 800-374-7747

Korean Air *www.koreanair.com* 800-438-5000

Lufthansa *www.lufthansa.com* 800-645-3880

Qantas Airways *www.qantas.com* 800-227-4500

South African Airways *www.flysaa.com* 800-722-9675

Swiss *www.swiss.com* 877-359-7947

Virgin Atlantic *www.virgin-atlantic.com* 800-862-8621

AUTOMOBILE RENTALS

Alamo Rent-A-Car *www.alamo.com* 800-327-9633

Avis Rent-A-Car *www.avis.com* 800-331-1212

Budget Rent-A-Car *www.budget.com* 800-527-0700

Dollar Rent-A-Car *www.dollar.com* 800-800-4000

Hertz Rent-A-Car *www.hertz.com* 800-654-3131

National Car Rental *www.nationalcar.com* ... 800-CAR-RENT

Thrifty Car Rental *www.thrifty.com* 800-367-2277

HOTELS AND MOTELS

Best Western Motels *www.bestwestern.com* 800-528-1234

Comfort Inns *www.comfortinn.com* 800-424-6423

Days Inns *www.daysinn.com* 800-329-7466

Doubletree Hotels *www.doubletree.com* 800-222-8733

Econo Lodges *www.econolodge.com* 877-424-6423

Embassy Suites *www.embassysuites.com* 800-EMBASSY

Fiesta Americana *www.fiestaamericana.com* ... 800-FIESTA-1

Hampton Inns *www.hampton-inn.com* 800-HAMPTON

Hilton Hotels *www.hilton.com* 800-445-8667

Holiday Inns *www.6c.com* 800-465-4329

Hotel InterContinental *www.interconti.com* 800-327-0200

Howard Johnson *www.hojo.com* 800-654-2000

Hyatt Hotels *www.hyatt.com* 800-233-1234

Marriott Hotels *www.marriott.com* 800-228-9290

Radisson Hotels *www.radisson.com* 800-333-3333

Ramada Inns *www.ramada.com* 800-2RAMADA

Red Carpet Inns *www.bookroomsnow.com* 800-251-1962

Red Lion Hotels & Inns *www.redlion.com* 800-547-8010

Renaissance Hotels *www.renaissancehotels.com* 888-236-2427

Resorts International *www.resorts-international.com* 800-336-6378

Sheraton Hotels & Inns *www.starwood.com* 800-325-3535

Sonesta International Hotels *www.sonesta.com* 800-766-3782

Travel Lodge *www.travelodge.com* 800-578-7878

Westin Hotels *www.starwood.com* 800-228-3000

Anniversary Gifts, Birthstones/Flowers, Holidays

ANNIVERSARY GIFTS

YEAR	TRADITIONAL	MODERN
1st	Paper	Clocks
2nd	Cotton	China
3rd	Leather	Crystal, Glass
4th	Books	Appliances
5th	Wood	Silverware
6th	Candy, Iron	Wood
7th	Wool, Copper	Desk Sets
8th	Bronze, Pottery	Linens, Lace
9th	Pottery, Willow	Leather
10th	Tin, Aluminum	Diamond Jewelry
11th	Steel	Fashion Jewelry
12th	Silk, Linen	Pearls
13th	Lace	Textiles, Furs
14th	Ivory	Gold Jewelry
15th	Crystal	Watches
20th	China	Platinum
25th	Silver	Silver
30th	Pearl	Diamond
35th	Coral	Jade
40th	Ruby	Ruby
50th	Gold	Gold
55th	Emerald	Emerald
60th	Diamond	Diamond
75th	Diamond	Diamond

BIRTHSTONES/FLOWERS

MONTH	STONE	FLOWER
January	Garnet	Carnation
February	Amethyst	Violet
March	Bloodstone	Jonquil
April	Diamond	Sweet Pea
May	Emerald	Lily of the Valley
June	Pearl	Rose
July	Ruby	Larkspur
August	Sardonyx	Gladiolus
September	Sapphire	Aster
October	Opal	Calendula
November	Topaz	Chrysanthemum
December	Turquoise	Narcissus

HOLIDAYS 2005

New Year's Day	January 1
Martin Luther King, Jr., Day	January 17
Groundhog Day	February 2
Ash Wednesday	February 9
Lincoln's Birthday	February 12
Valentine's Day	February 14
Presidents' Day	February 21
Washington's Birthday	February 22
St. Patrick's Day	March 17
First Day of Spring	March 20
Palm Sunday	March 20
Good Friday	March 25
Easter Sunday	March 27
April Fool's Day	April 1
Daylight Saving Time begins	April 3
Passover begins at sundown	April 23
National Arbor Day	April 29
Mother's Day	May 8
Armed Forces Day (U.S.)	May 21
Victoria Day (Canada)	May 24
Memorial Day (observed)	May 30
Flag Day	June 14
Father's Day	June 19
First Day of Summer	June 21
Canada Day	July 1
Independence Day (U.S.)	July 4
Labor Day	September 5
First Day of Autumn	September 22
Rosh Hashanah begins at sundown	October 3
Ramadan begins	October 3
Columbus Day (observed)	October 10
Thanksgiving Day (Canada)	October 10
Yom Kippur begins at sundown	October 12
Daylight Saving Time ends	October 30
Halloween	October 31
Veterans Day	November 11
Thanksgiving Day (U.S.)	November 24
First Day of Winter	December 21
Hanukkah begins at sundown	December 25
Christmas Day	December 25
Boxing Day (Canada)	December 26
Kwanzaa begins	December 26
New Year's Eve	December 31

Notes

Notes

Notes

Notes

Compiled by Dara N. Byrne, Ph.D., and Adrienne Ingrum

Designed by Shonna Dowers

Cover painting: *Civil Rights Protesters at the 1964 Democratic National Convention* by Franklin McMahon, © Franklin McMahon/CORBIS

Black Expressions 2005 Calendar is a publication of Black Expressions Book Club, 401 Franklin Avenue, Garden City, NY 11530.

ISBN: 1-58288-144-8

Printed in the United States of America